Robin Hood
and His Merry Outlaws

RETOLD FROM THE OLD BALLADS

by

J. Walker McSpadden

CORE CLASSICS®

SERIES EDITOR MICHAEL J. MARSHALL

EDITED AND ABRIDGED BY MICHAEL J. MARSHALL

LIBRARY OF CONGRESS CATALOG CARD NUMBER: 00-107525

ISBN 978-1-890517-16-8 TRADE PAPERBACK

COPYRIGHT © 2000 CORE KNOWLEDGE FOUNDATION

ALL RIGHTS RESERVED · PRINTED IN CANADA

THIS PRINTING, JULY 2011

DESIGNED BY BILL WOMACK INCORPORATED

COVER ILLUSTRATION BY GB McINTOSH

TEXT ILLUSTRATIONS BY LOUIS RHEAD

CORE KNOWLEDGE FOUNDATION

801 EAST HIGH STREET

CHARLOTTESVILLE, VIRGINIA 22902

www.coreknowledge.org

TABLE · of · CONTENTS

TWO HEROES FROM THE MIDDLE AGES still stir our imaginations. One is King Arthur, with his knights of the Round Table. The other is Robin Hood, with his band of forest outlaws. King Arthur and his knights live at court. They go into the dark woods when they are after adventure. But forests hold no danger for Robin Hood and his men. Sherwood Forest is their home, and they feel safe there. The King Arthur stories tell of the mighty noblemen who rule. The Robin Hood stories tell of common men who defy their masters and rule themselves.

Was Robin Hood a real person? Probably not. But English records from the Middle Ages do tell of desperate criminals who ran into the woods to hide from the law and lived in bands, robbing those who passed through their gloomy glens.

The Robin Hood stories come to us from ballads popular in the 13th century. A ballad is a song or poem that usually tells a story. Ballads have rhyming four-line stanzas, sometimes followed by a chorus. You'll find verses from these old ballads introducing each chapter of our story.

The Robin Hood ballads were also performed as skits. In the 1400s, towns across England held games and plays in Robin Hood's name. In early summer a procession of villagers led by someone dressed as Robin Hood went to a neighboring village, where they performed a skit. Usually it showed how Robin Hood made a daring rescue. They collected money for their performance and spent it on such things as road repair.

Robin Hood became a popular hero because he represented the ordinary person's desire to be treated fairly. Medieval society had three ranks: the nobility, the men of the church and, lastly, common folk. The nobles were responsible for worldly welfare and the churchmen for spiritual welfare. That is, the duty of the nobility was to defend Christian lands with their lives. The duty of the clergy was to shepherd souls toward heaven and plead for God's blessings. The duty of common men was to keep everyone fed.

As the leaders of Christianity, nobles and clergy

should have acted in Christian ways toward the common people. They should have treated them with love, charity and goodness and, of course, according to the law. But what powerful men declare to be the law is not necessarily what either religious faith or fair reasoning would call justice. Thus it often happened that the common people hated their local authorities and grumbled against anyone who enjoyed luxuries. Robin Hood rejects unjust laws, seeing them as the will of wicked and greedy men.

To get away from the power of the sheriff and the bishop, Robin Hood and his outlaws live outdoors in Sherwood Forest. Their warm fellowship is based on equality. The outlaws choose Robin as their chief because his daring wins their admiration and loyalty. They believe they obey a higher law than the sheriff's law, one that respects the dignity of every person. They feel justified in resisting their rulers because their rulers are not following that higher law. Robin Hood is devoted to the Virgin Mary, for example, but not to the church, because church leaders were not following their own teachings. He honors the idea of his king, but he believes the king's deer really belong to the hungriest poor folk. He does not object to wealth or rank, but to the wrong use of those advantages. His remedy for the suffering of the weak is to steal from the rich to give to the poor. Only those whose wealth is unearned need to fear Robin or his outlaws. Even then, rich travelers who tell Robin the truth get to keep some money. Those who lie lose it all.

Proving that many distinctions society makes between the high and the low ranks are false, Robin Hood shows that chivalry, the medieval code of courtesy and courage that guided behavior at King Arthur's court, can guide a common man's life as well. Robin Hood holds court in the forest just as King Arthur does at Camelot. Just as chivalry required every knight to defend and respect every woman, Robin Hood forbids any of his outlaws ever to hurt a woman, or any man if a woman is present. He demands loyalty, honesty and courage from each man, just as Arthur expects from his knights. Robin's word is his bond, even to his enemies, and he is careful never to tell lies, even as he plays tricks. He lives by the rules of honor as much as does Sir Lancelot, the most illustrious knight of King Arthur's Round Table.

Robin is a natural leader, bold and shrewd, but he is not the best of his band at anything except archery. To the outlaws of Sherwood Forest, skill at archery is their special badge. Their long bows stood about six feet tall and could send an arrow the length of three football fields. At close range, those arrows could even go through armor. English archers became famous throughout Europe after their long bows won victories against the French at the battles of Crécy and Agincourt in the Hundred Years' War. English kings understood the value of expert archers and held tournaments to encourage the skill. Robin cannot resist the chance a tournament gives to show his amazing aim, even though to go means he risks hanging. This gallant spirit, equal to any of King Arthur's knights, and his common-sense fairness have made Robin Hood our favorite outlaw for more than 700 years.

E. D. HIRSCH JR.

CHARLOTTESVILLE, VIRGINIA

Robin Hood and His Merry Outlaws

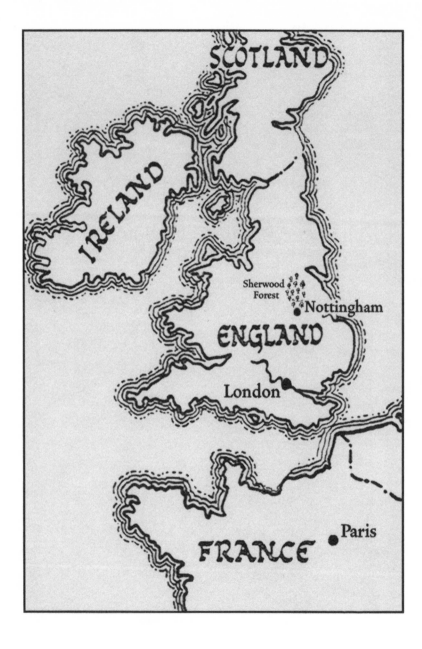

CHAPTER 1

How Robin Hood Became an Outlaw

"List and hearken, gentlemen,
    That be of freeborn blood,
I shall you tell of a good **yeoman**,
    His name was Robin Hood.

Robin was a proud outlaw,
    While as he walked on the ground:
So courteous an outlaw as he was one
    Was never none else found."

I N THE DAYS OF KING HARRY the Second of
England there were certain forests in the
North Country set aside for the King's
hunting. Any man who shot a deer in them
faced the penalty of death. These forests were

YEOMAN
A man who works his own small farm.

1

guarded by the King's Foresters, the chief of whom, in each wood, was equal in authority to the sheriff in his walled town, or even to a bishop in his **abbey**.

One of the greatest of the royal hunting preserves was Sherwood Forest, near the town of Nottingham. Here for some years lived one Hugh Fitzooth as Head Forester, with his wife and little son Robert. The boy had been born in Lockesley town in the year 1160, records say, and was often called Lockesley, or Rob of Lockesley. He was a handsome, well-built boy, and as soon as he was strong enough to walk, his chief delight was to go with his father into the forest. As soon as his right arm grew strong enough, he learned to draw the **long bow** and shoot a true arrow. On winter evenings his greatest joy was to hear his father tell of Will o' the Green, the bold outlaw who for many summers defied the King's Foresters and feasted with his men upon King's deer. And on stormy days the boy learned to whittle out a straight

ABBEY
Several buildings including a church, where men or women lived a religious life.

LONG BOW
A wooden bow about six feet long. It was so effective that English archers using them defeated mounted French knights in the two major battles of the Hundred Years' War, Crécy (1346) and Agincourt (1415).

shaft for the long bow and fit it with grey goose feathers.

His loving mother sighed when she saw the boy's face light up at these woodland tales. She was of **gentle birth**, and had hoped to see her son famous at the king's court or in the bishop's abbey. She taught him to read and to write, to lift his cap gracefully, and to answer directly and truthfully both lord and peasant. But the boy, although he took kindly to these lessons, was happiest when he had his beloved bow in hand and wandered freely, listening to the murmur of the trees.

GENTLE BIRTH
Someone born into the gentry; landholders lower than the highest class, the nobility.

Rob had two playmates in those early days. One was Will Gamewell, his father's brother's son, who lived at Gamewell Lodge, very near Nottingham town. The other was Marian Fitzwalter, only child of the Earl of Huntingdon, whose castle could be seen from the top of one of the tall trees in Sherwood. On more than one bright day Rob's white signal from this tree told Marian that he awaited her there. Rob did not visit her at the castle. His father and her father were enemies. Some people whispered that Hugh Fitzooth was the rightful Earl of Huntingdon, but that he had been cheated out of his lands by Fitzwalter, who had won the King's favor by a **Crusade** to the Holy Land. But Rob or Marian cared little for this hatred, however it had begun. They knew that the great greenwood was open to them, and it was full of the scent of flowers and the song of birds.

Days of youth passed all too swiftly, and troubled skies came all too soon. Rob's father had two other enemies besides Fitzwalter: the lean Sheriff of Nottingham and the fat Bishop of Hereford. These three enemies one day got to the King's ear, and whispered in it to such evil purpose that the King removed Hugh Fitzooth from his post of King's Forester. He and his wife and Rob, then a youth of nineteen, were evicted on a cold winter's evening, empty-handed, without warning. The Sheriff arrested the Forester for **treason**, of which, poor man, he was as guiltless as you or I, and carried him to Nottingham jail. Rob and his mother stayed overnight in the jail also, but the next morning they were

CRUSADE
"War of the Cross"; a series of wars from 1096 to 1291 in which European Christians fought Muslims to control Jerusalem and the Holy Land.

TREASON
The crime of betraying your country, or trying to overthrow its government.

roughly told to go about their business. They turned for shelter to their only kinsman, Squire George of Gamewell, who kindly took them in.

But the shock and the winter night's journey proved too much for Rob's mother. She had not been strong for some time before leaving the forest. In less than two months she was no more. Rob felt as though his heart were broken. But scarcely had the first spring flowers begun to blossom upon her grave when he had another crushing blow—the loss of his father. That brave man died in prison before his accusers could agree upon the charges on which he was to be brought to trial.

Two years passed by. Rob's cousin Will was away at school. And Marian's father, who had learned of her friendship with Rob, had sent his daughter to the court of Queen Eleanor. So these years were lonely ones to the orphaned lad. The bluff old Squire was kind to him but secretly could not understand someone who went about brooding, as though seeking for something he had lost. The truth is that Rob missed his old life in the forest no less than his mother's gentleness and his father's companionship. Every time he twanged the string of the long bow against his shoulder and heard the grey goose shaft sing, it told him of happy days that he could not bring back.

One morning as Rob came in to breakfast, his uncle greeted him with: "I have news for you, Rob, my lad!" and the hearty old Squire set his pewter tankard of ale down with a crash.

"What may that be, Uncle Gamewell?" asked the young man.

"Here is a chance to exercise your good long bow and win a pretty prize. The Fair is on at Nottingham, and the Sheriff proclaims an archers' tournament. The best fellows are to have places with the King's Foresters, and the one who shoots straightest of all will win a golden arrow, a useless bauble, but just the thing for your lady love, eh, Rob, my boy?" The Squire laughed and whacked the table again with his tankard.

Rob's eyes sparkled. "'Tis indeed worth shooting for, uncle," he said. "And a place among the Foresters is what I have long desired. Will you let me try?"

"To be sure," rejoined his uncle. "I know that your good mother would want me to make a clerk of you; but I see very well that the greenwood is where you will pass your days, so here's luck to you!" And the huge tankard came down a third time.

Yovng·Robin·goes·to the·Shooting·Match·

One fine morning a few days after, Rob passed briskly and gaily through Sherwood Forest to Nottingham. His hopes were high and he had no enemy in the wide world. But it was the very last morning in all his life when he lacked an enemy. As he went on his way, whistling, he came suddenly upon a group of Foresters beneath the spreading branches of an oak tree. They had a meat pie and were washing down huge slices of it with brown ale.

When he glanced at the leader, Rob knew at once that he had found an enemy. It was the man who had taken his father's place as Head Forester and roughly turned his mother out in the snow. But Robin said not a word, for good or bad, and would have passed on his way. But this man, clearing his throat with a huge gulp of ale, bellowed out: "My word, here is a pretty little archer! Where are you going, lad, with that toy bow and arrows? To shoot at Nottingham Fair? Ho! Ho! Ho!"

Rob flushed, for he was very proud of his shooting.

"My bow is as good as yours," he answered, "and my shafts will carry as straight and as far, so I'll not take lessons from any of you!"

They laughed again loudly at this, and the leader said, with a frown:

"Show us your skill, and if you can hit the mark here's twenty silver pennies for you, but if you miss you are in for a sound beating for your sassiness."

"Pick your own target," said Rob in a rage. "I'll lay my head against that purse that I can hit it."

"As you say," answered the Forester angrily. "Your head if you cannot hit my target."

Now at a little rise in the wood, a herd of deer came by grazing, a full hundred yards away. They were the King's deer, but at that distance seemed safe from any harm. The Head Forester pointed to them.

"If your young arm could send a shaft for half that distance I'd shoot with you."

"Done!" cried Rob. "My head against twenty pennies I'll cause the fine fellow in the lead of them to breathe his last."

And without more ado he tried the string of his long bow, placed a shaft on it, and drew it to his ear. A moment later the quivering string sang death as the shaft whistled across the glade. Then the leader of the herd leaped high in his tracks and fell prone, staining the turf with his heart's blood.

A murmur of amazement swept through the Foresters, and then a growl of rage. He who made the wager was angriest of all.

"Do you know what you have done?" he said. "You have killed the King's deer. By the laws of King Harry you should pay with your head. Talk not of pennies, but get gone straight, and let me not look upon your face again."

Rob's blood boiled, and he said, rashly, "I have looked upon your face once too often already—you who wear my father's shoes."

And with this he turned and walked away.

The Forester heard these parting words and cursed. Red with rage, he seized his bow and without warning launched an arrow at Rob. Luckily for Rob, the Forester's foot turned on a twig at the critical instant. As it was, the arrow whizzed by his ear so closely that it took a stray strand of his hair with it.

Rob turned upon his attacker, now forty yards away.

"Ha!" said he. "You do not shoot as straight as I, for all your bravado. Take this from the toy bow!"

Straight flew his answering shaft. The Head Forester gave one cry, then fell face downward and lay still. His life avenged the death of Rob's father, but Rob was now outlawed. Forward he ran through the forest, before the band could gather their scattered wits, and the swaying trees of the great greenwood seemed to open their arms to welcome him home.

Later that same day, Rob paused, hungry and weary, at the cottage of a poor widow who lived on the outskirts of the forest. This widow had often greeted him kindly in his boyhood days, giving him things to eat and drink, so he boldly entered her door. The old woman was indeed glad to see him. She baked him cakes and had him rest and tell his story. Then she shook her head.

"An evil wind blows through Sherwood," she

said. "The poor are plundered, and the rich ride over their bodies. My three sons have been outlawed for shooting the King's deer to keep us from starving, and they now hide in the woods. They tell me that forty good men are in hiding with them."

"Where are they?" cried Rob. "By my faith, I will join them."

"Nay, nay," replied the old woman at first. But when she saw that there was no other way, she said: "My sons will visit me tonight. Stay here and see them if you must."

So Rob stayed to see the widow's sons that night, for they were men after his own heart. And when they found that his mood was with them, they made him swear an oath of loyalty and told him the hideaway of the band, a place he knew very well. Finally, one of them said:

"But the band lacks a leader, one who can use his head as well as his hands, so we have agreed that he who has skill enough to go to Nottingham as an outlaw and win the prize at archery shall be our chief."

Rob sprang to his feet. "I had started to that same Fair," he cried. "And all the Foresters and all the

Sheriff's men in Christendom shall not stand between me and the center of their target!"

His eye flashed with such fire that the three brothers seized his hand and shouted:

"A Lockesley! A Lockesley! If you win the golden arrow you shall be chief of outlaws in Sherwood Forest!"

So Rob began planning how he could disguise himself to go to Nottingham, for he knew that a price would be set on his head.

As Rob foresaw, in the marketplace the Sheriff of Nottingham posted a reward of two hundred pounds for the capture, dead or alive, of one Robert Fitzooth, outlaw. And the crowds thronging the streets upon that busy Fair day often paused to read the notice and talk together about the death of the Head Forester.

But a Fair day brought up so many other things to talk about that the reward was forgotten for the time being, and only the Foresters and Sheriff's men watched the gates closely.

The great event of the day came in the afternoon. It was the archers' contest for the golden arrow, and twenty men stepped forward to shoot. Among them was a beggar, a sorry looking fellow, with leggings of different

colors and brown, scratched face and hands. Over a
shock of light brown hair he had a hood drawn, like that
of a monk. Slowly he limped to his place in the line,
while the mob shouted mockery. But the contest was
open to all comers, so no man could stop him.

Beside Rob, for it was he who dressed as a beggar,
stood a muscular fellow with one eye hidden by a green
bandage. The crowd also jeered him, but he passed them
by with indifference.

All the gentry and people of the surrounding
country were gathered in eager expectancy. The central
box contained the lean but proud Sheriff, his bejeweled
wife, and their daughter, who, it was openly hinted, was
hoping to receive the golden arrow from the victor, and
so be crowned queen of the day.

Next to the Sheriff's box was one occupied by the
fat Bishop of Hereford. On the other side was a box
where sat a girl whose dark hair, dark eyes, and fair fea-
tures caused Rob's heart to leap. Maid Marian! She had
come up for a visit from the Queen's court at London and
now sat by her father, the Earl of Huntingdon. The sight
of her sweet face multiplied Rob's determination a hundred times. He felt his muscles tightening. Yet, despite

this, his heart throbbed, making him quake in a most strange way.

Then the trumpet sounded, and the crowd became silent while the herald announced the rules of the contest. It was open to all comers. The first target was to be placed thirty yards away, and all those who hit its center were allowed to shoot at the second target, placed ten yards farther off. The third target was to be moved yet farther, until the winner was proved. The winner was to receive the golden arrow and a place with the King's Foresters. He would also crown the queen of the day.

The trumpet sounded again, and the archers prepared to shoot. Twelve out of the twenty contestants reached the inner circle of the first target. Rob shot sixth in the line and hit the center squarely. He heard an approving grunt from the man with the green eye patch, who shot next, and carelessly, yet true to the bull's-eye.

The mob cheered and yelled themselves hoarse at even this marksmanship. The trumpet sounded again, and a new target was set up forty yards away.

The first three archers again struck true, amid loud applause, for they were expected to win. Indeed, it was whispered that each was backed by one of the three dignitaries of the day: the Sheriff, the Bishop, and the Earl. The fourth and fifth archers barely grazed the center. Rob fitted his arrow quietly and with confidence sped it straight toward the shining circle.

"The beggar!" yelled the crowd. "Another bull's-eye for the beggar!"

In truth his shaft was nearer the center than any of the others'. But it was not so near that "Blinder," as the mob had nicknamed his neighbor, did not place his shaft just within the mark. Again the crowd cheered wildly. Shooting such as this was not seen every day.

The other archers in this round missed one after another. They dropped moodily back while the trumpet sounded for the third round, and the target was set up fifty yards distant.

"You draw a good bow," said Rob's comrade to him in the interval allowed for rest. "Do you wish me to shoot first this time?"

"Nay," said Rob, "but you are a good fellow to offer, and if I do not win I hope you can keep the prize from those strutters." And he nodded scornfully to the three other archers, who were surrounded by their admirers. Then his eye wandered toward Maid Marian's booth. She had been watching him, it seemed, for their eyes met; then she looked away.

"Blinder's" quick eye followed Rob's. "A fair maid, that," he said smiling. "And one more worthy of the golden arrow than the Sheriff's proud daughter."

Rob looked at him swiftly, but saw only kindness in his glance. "You are a shrewd fellow, and I like you well," was all he said.

Now the archers prepared to shoot again. The target seemed hardly larger than the inner ring had looked at the first trial. The first three sped their shafts, and though they were good shots, they only grazed the inner circle.

Rob took his turn with some worry. Some scattered clouds overhead made the light uncertain, and a wind gusted across the range. His eyes wandered for a brief moment to the box where the dark-eyed girl sat. His heart leaped! She met his glance and smiled at him. And in that moment he felt that she knew him despite his disguise and looked to him to keep the honor of old Sherwood. He drew his bow firmly and, taking advantage of a lull in the breeze, launched the arrow straight and true to the center of the target.

"The beggar! A bull's-eye! A bull's-eye!" yelled the fickle mob. "Can you beat that, Blinder?"

The last archer smiled scornfully, drew his bow with ease and grace, and, without seeming to study the course, released the winged arrow. All eyes followed its flight. A loud uproar broke forth when it hit just outside the center, grazing the shaft sent by Rob. The stranger made a gesture of surprise when his own eyes showed the result to him, but saw his error. He had not allowed for the wind, which carried the arrow to one side. Still, he was the first to congratulate Rob.

"I hope we may shoot again," he said. "In truth, I do not care for the golden bauble and wished to win it to spite the Sheriff. Now crown the lady of your choice." And, turning suddenly, he was lost in the crowd before Rob could utter what was on his lips to say, that he hoped to shoot with him again.

The herald summoned Rob to the Sheriff's box to receive the prize.

"You are a curious fellow," said the Sheriff, biting his lip coldly, "yet you shoot well. What name do you go by?"

Marian sat near, listening intently.

"I am called Rob the Stroller, my Lord Sheriff," said the archer.

Marian leaned back and smiled.

"Well, Rob the Stroller, with a little attention to your skin and clothes you would not be so bad a man," said the Sheriff. "How do you like the idea of entering my service?"

"Rob the Stroller has always been a free man, my Lord, and desires no service."

The Sheriff's brow darkened, yet for the sake of his daughter he concealed his feelings.

"Rob the Stroller," said he, "here is the golden arrow which is meant for the best archer this day. You are awarded the prize. Bestow it worthily."

At this point the herald nudged Rob and half nodded his head toward the Sheriff's daughter, who sat with a thin smile on her lips. But Rob took the arrow to the next box, where Maid Marian sat.

"Lady," he said, "pray accept this little pledge from a poor stroller who would devote himself to your service."

"My thanks to you, Rob in the Hood," she replied, with a twinkle in her eye; and she placed the gleaming arrow in her hair, while the people shouted: "The Queen! The Queen!"

The Sheriff looked furiously at this ragged archer who had refused his offer of a job, taken his prize without a word of thanks, and snubbed his daughter. He would have spoken, but his proud daughter restrained him. He called to his guard and told them to watch the beggar. But Rob had already lost himself in the crowd and was headed straight for the town gate.

That evening in a forest glade, a group of men clad in **Lincoln green** sat round a fire roasting venison. Suddenly a twig crackled, and they sprang to their feet and seized their weapons.

"I look for the widow's sons," a clear voice said, "and I come alone."

LINCOLN GREEN
A color of wool cloth once made in Lincoln, England.

Instantly the three men stepped forward.

"Rob!" they cried. "Welcome to Sherwood Forest!" And all the men greeted him, for they had heard his story.

Then one of the widow's sons, Stout Will, stepped forward, and said:

"Comrades all, ye know that our band has sadly

lacked a leader. We may have found that leader in this young man. And I and my brothers have told him that you would choose that one who would bring the Sheriff to shame this day and capture his golden arrow. Is it not so?"

The band agreed, and Will turned to Rob. "What news do you bring from Nottingham?" asked he.

Rob laughed. "To tell the truth, I brought the Sheriff to shame for my own pleasure and won his golden arrow to boot. But as to the prize, you must take my word, for I gave it to a maid."

Seeing the men doubted this, he continued: "But I'll gladly join your band as a common archer. For there are others older and perhaps more skilled than I."

Then one stepped forward from the rest, a tall swarthy man, and Rob recognised him as the man with the green patch, only it was now removed.

"Rob in the Hood, for such the lady called you," said he, "I can vouch for your tale. You shamed the Sheriff as I had hoped to do, and the golden arrow is indeed in fair hands. As to your shooting and mine, we must let future days decide. But here I, Will Stutely, declare that I will serve no other chief but you."

Then Will Stutely told the outlaws of Rob's deeds and gave him his hand in loyalty. The widow's sons did likewise, as did the other members, every one, gladly, because Will Stutely had heretofore been the truest bow in all the company. They toasted him with ale and hailed him as their leader by the name of Robin Hood. And he accepted that name because Maid Marian had said it.

By the light of the campfire the band exchanged signs and passwords. They gave Robin Hood a horn to blow to summon them. They swore, also, that while they might take money and goods from the unjust rich, they would aid the poor and the helpless, and that they would harm no woman. They swore all this with solemn oaths, while they feasted about the ruddy blaze, under the greenwood tree.

And that is how Robin Hood became an outlaw.

CHAPTER 2

How Robin Hood Met Little John

⌒✱⌒

"'O here is my hand,' the stranger replied,
   'I'll serve you with all my whole heart:
My name is John Little, a man of good **mettle**;
   Never doubt me for I'll play my part.'

'His name shall be altered,' said William Stutely,
   'And I will his godfather be:
Prepare then a feast, and none of the least,
   For we will be merry,' said he."

⌒✱⌒

ALL THAT SUMMER ROBIN HOOD and his merry men roamed in Sherwood Forest, and the fame of their deeds spread abroad in the land. The Sheriff of Nottingham raged over the outlaws, but all his traps and searches

METTLE
An attitude of courage and endurance.

22

failed to catch them. The poor people first feared them, but when they found that Robin Hood's men meant them no harm, but took from the rich and gave to the poor, they began to have a great liking for them. The band increased, till by the end of the summer eighty men had sworn loyalty.

But the quiet days seemed dull to Robin's adventurous spirit. One morning, he rose and slung his quiver over his shoulder.

"This fresh breeze stirs the blood, lads," said he, "and I want to see what the world looks like in the direction of Nottingham. But you tarry behind in the borders of the forest, within earshot of my bugle call."

Thus saying, he strode merrily forward to the edge of the wood and paused there a moment, his agile body erect, his brown locks flowing, and his brown eyes watching the road.

The highway was clear in the direction of the town. But at a bend in the road he turned onto a path leading across a brook, which made the way shorter and less open. As he approached the stream, he saw that it had become swollen by recent rains into quite a torrent. The log footbridge was still there, but he had no sooner started across than he saw a tall stranger coming from the other side. Robin quickened his pace, and the stranger did likewise, each thinking to cross first. They met at the middle of the log, and neither would yield an inch.

"Give way, fellow!" roared Robin.

The stranger smiled. He was almost a head taller than Robin. "Nay!" he retorted, "I give way only to a better man than myself."

"Give way, I say," repeated Robin, "or I shall have to show you a better man."

His opponent budged not an inch, but laughed loudly. "Now," he said goodnaturedly, "I'll not move after hearing that speech, even if I might have before. I have sought this better man my whole life long. Therefore show him to me."

"That will I right soon," said Robin. "Stay here while I cut a cudgel like that you have been twiddling in your fingers." So saying, he leapt to his own bank again, laid aside his long bow and arrows, and cut a stout staff of oak, a good six feet in length. Still, it was a full foot shorter than his opponent's. Then back he came boldly.

"I do not mind telling you, fellow," said he, "that

an archery match would have been an easier way for me. But there are other tunes in England besides those an arrow sings." Then he whirled the staff above his head. "So make ready for the tune I am about to play upon your ribs! One! Two!"

"Three!" roared the giant, striking at him instantly.

Fortunately for Robin he was quick and nimble, for the blow that grazed his shoulder would have felled an ox. Nevertheless, while swerving to avoid this stroke, Robin was preparing for his own, and back he came with a whack!

Whack! parried the other.

Whack! Whack! Whack! Whack!

The fight was fast and furious. It was strength pitted against skill. The mighty blows of the stranger went whistling around Robin's ducking head, while his own swift undercuts give the stranger an attack of indigestion. Yet each stood firmly in his place, not moving backward or forward a foot for a good half hour. The giant's face was getting red, and his breath came snorting forth like a bull's. Robin dodged his blows lightly, then sprang in swiftly and unexpectedly and gave the

Robin Hood · meeteth · the · tall
Stranger · on · the · Bridge

stranger a wicked blow upon the ribs.

The stranger reeled and nearly fell, but regained his footing.

"By my life, you can hit hard!" he gasped, giving back a blow as he staggered.

That blow was a lucky one. It caught Robin off his guard. His stick had rested a moment while he looked to see the giant topple into the water, when down came a whack on his head that dropped Robin neatly into the stream.

The cool, rushing current quickly brought him to his senses. But he was still so dazed that he groped blindly for the swaying reeds to pull himself up on the bank. His opponent could not help laughing heartily, but he also thrust down his long staff to Robin, crying: "Lay hold of that!"

Robin took hold and was hauled to dry land like a fish. He lay upon the warm bank for a while to regain his senses; then he sat up and rubbed his head.

"By all the saints!" said he. "My head hums like a beehive on a summer morning."

Then he picked up his horn, which lay near, and blew three shrill notes that echoed among the trees. A moment of silence followed, then the rustling of leaves and crackling of twigs could be heard, and from the glade two dozen yeomen burst, all clad in Lincoln green like Robin, with Will Stutely and the widow's three sons at their head.

"Good master," cried Will Stutely, "how is this? There is not a dry thread on you."

"This fellow would not let me pass the foot-bridge," replied Robin, "and when I tickled him in the ribs he answered with a pat on my head that sent me in the stream."

"Then shall he taste some of his own porridge," said Will. "Seize him, lads!"

"Nay, let him go free," said Robin. "The fight was a fair one. Are you ready to quit?" he continued, turning to the stranger with a twinkling eye.

"I am content," said the other, "for I like you well and wish to know your name."

"My men, and even the Sheriff of Nottingham, know me as Robin Hood, the outlaw."

"Then I am right sorry that I beat you," exclaimed the man, "for I was on my way to join your company. But now that I have used my staff on you I fear you will not have me."

"Nay, never say it!" cried Robin, "I am glad you fell in with me, though I did all the falling!"

As the others laughed, the two men clasped hands, and the strong friendship of a lifetime began.

"But you have not told us your name," said Robin.

"Where I came from, men call me John Little."

"Enter our company, then, John Little, and welcome. All we ask is your whole mind and body and heart even unto death."

"I give the bond, on my life," said the tall man.

Then Will Stutely, who loved a good joke, spoke up and said: "The infant in our household must be christened, and I'll be his godfather. This stranger is so small of bone and muscle that his old name does not suit the purpose." Here Will paused long enough to fill a horn in the stream, and then he stood on tiptoe to splash the water on the giant: "I christen you Little John."

At this the men roared long and loud.

"A bow and a full sheath of arrows for Little John," said Robin joyfully. "Can you shoot as well as you fight with the staff, my friend?"

"I have hit an ash twig at forty yards," said Little John.

Thus chatting pleasantly the band turned back into the woodland and toward their hideaway, where the trees were the thickest, the moss was the softest, and a secret path led to a cave that was both safe and a **stronghold**. Here under a mighty oak they found the rest of the band with two fat does. And here they built a fire and sat down to the meat and ale, Robin Hood in the center, with Will Stutely on the one hand and Little John on the other. Robin was happy with the day's adventure, even though he had got a drubbing; for sore ribs and heads will heal, and it's not every day that one can find a friend as true as Little John.

STRONG-HOLD
A fort.

CHAPTER 3

How Robin Hood Turned Butcher and Entered the Sheriff's Service

*"The butcher he answered jolly Robin,
'No matter where I do dwell,
For a butcher am I, and to Nottingham
Am I going, my meat to sell.'"*

T HREE DAYS LATER one of Will Stutely's fellows struck down a fine stag. As he and others had stepped from cover to seize it, twenty of the Sheriff's men appeared at the end of the glade. Will's men dropped down on all fours, barely in time to hear a shower of arrows whistle above their heads. Then from behind the trees they sent back such an answer that the

Sheriff's men would come no closer. Two of them, in truth, took unpleasant wounds in their shoulders from the encounter.

When they returned to town the Sheriff turned red with rage.

"What," he gasped, "do my men fear to fight this Robin Hood face to face? If only I could get him within my reach once. We would see then!"

What it was the Sheriff would see he did not say. But soon he had his wish granted.

The next day and the one following, Little John was missing. One of the men said that he saw him talking with a beggar, but did not know where they had gone. Two more days passed. Robin grew uneasy. He feared the King's Foresters had captured Little John.

At last Robin could not remain quiet. Up he sprang, with bow and arrows, and a short sword at his side.

"I must go to Nottingham," he cried. "The Sheriff has long desired to see me; and perhaps he can tell me news of the best **quarterstaff** in the **shire**"—meaning Little John.

Others asked to go with him, but he would not let them.

QUARTERSTAFF
A long, strong wooden stick used as a weapon.

SHIRE
An English county.

"Nay," he said, "but tarry in the edge of the wood opposite the west gate of the town, and you may be of service tomorrow night."

So saying he went to the road leading to Nottingham and stood as before, looking up and down to see if the way were clear. Back at a bend in the road he heard a rumbling, when up drove a stout butcher, whistling gaily and driving a horse that walked slowly because of the weight of meat loaded in the cart.

"Good day to you, friend," hailed Robin. "Where are you going with your load of meat?"

"Good day to you," returned the butcher. "I am but a simple butcher on my way to Nottingham. 'Tis Fair week, and my beef and mutton will bring a fair penny. But who are you?"

"Men call me Robin Hood."

"The saints protect me!" said the butcher in terror. "I heard of you and how you lighten the purses of the fat priests and knights. But I am only but a poor butcher, selling this load of meat, perhaps for enough to pay my rent."

"Rest, my friend, rest," said Robin. "I would not take as much as a penny from you, for I love an honest face and a good name with my neighbors. But I would strike a bargain."

He took a well-filled purse from his belt and continued. "I would like to be a butcher today and sell meat at Nottingham. Could you sell me your meat, your cart, your horse, and your goodwill for five gold pieces?"

"Heaven bless ye, good Robin," cried the butcher joyfully, "that can I!" And he leaped down from the cart and handed Robin the reins in exchange for the purse.

"One moment more," laughed Robin. "We must change garments for the time being. Take mine and scurry home, lest the King's Foresters try to put a hole through this Lincoln green."

So he donned the butcher's shirt and apron and drove to the town.

When he came to Nottingham, he went to the

marketplace. Boldly he led his shuffling horse to where the butchers had their stalls. He had no notion of the price to ask for his meat, but thus he called aloud:

> *"Hark ye, lasses and dames, hark ye,*
> *Good meat come buy, come buy;*
> *Three pennies' worth go for one penny,*
> *And a kiss is good, say I!"*

People crowded round his cart, for he really did sell three times as much for one penny as was sold by the other butchers. And one or two lasses liked his face so well that they willingly gave him a kiss.

But the other butchers were angry when they found how he was taking their trade, and so they put their heads together.

One said: "Perhaps he has sold his father's land and this is his first try at trading."

Another said: "Perhaps he has murdered a butcher and stolen his horse and meat."

Robin heard these sayings, but only laughed and sang his song louder. The people laughed also and crowded round his cart closely, shouting uproariously

Robin·turns·butcher·and·
sells·his·meat·in·Nottingham:

when some lass agreed to be kissed.

Then the butchers said to him: "Come, brother butcher, if you would sell meat with us you must join our **guild** and go by the rules of our trade."

"We dine at the Sheriff's mansion today," said another, "and you must be one of us."

"I'll go with you, my brothers," said jolly Robin, "and as fast as I can."

Then, having sold all his meat, he left his horse and cart in the care of a friendly innkeeper and followed the butchers to the mansion.

GUILD
An association formed by merchants or craftsmen to control trade in a product or service. Each chose a symbol of its trade.

It was the Sheriff's custom to host guilds of the trades from time to time on Fair days, for he got a pretty profit out of the fees they paid him for the right to trade in the marketplace. The Sheriff had already come into the banqueting room with great pomp when Robin Hood and three or four butchers entered.

The Sheriff motioned Robin to sit by his right hand at the head of the table, for one or two butchers had whispered to him: "That fellow is mad. He sold more meat for one penny than we could sell for three, and he

gave extra weight to any lass who would kiss him."
Others said: "He does not know the value of goods and
may be cheated by a shrewd man."

The Sheriff was willing to cheat any man, and he
was glad to have a guest who promised to enliven the
feast. So he made much of Robin and laughed loudly at
his jests, though, to tell the truth, the laugh came easily,
for Robin had never been in a merrier mood, and his
jests soon put the whole table in a roar.

Then the lord Bishop of Hereford came in, last of
all, to say grace and take his seat on the other side of the
Sheriff.

After grace was said, and while the servants clat-
tered in with meat platters, Robin stood up and said:

"Amen, I say, to my lord Bishop's thanks! Now,
my fine fellows, be merry and drink deep, for I'll pay for
all before I go my way, though it cost me five pounds and
more. So spare not the wine."

"Hear! Hear!" shouted the butchers.

"Now are you a jolly soul," said the Sheriff, "but
this feast is mine. You must have many head of cattle and
many acres of broad land, to spend so freely."

"Aye, that I have," returned Robin. "My brothers

and I have five hundred head, and none of them have we been able to sell. That is why I have turned butcher. But I do not know the trade and would gladly sell the whole herd, if I could find a buyer."

At this the Sheriff's greed began to rise.

"Five hundred head, you say?"

"Five hundred and ten, by actual count, that I would sell for twenty pieces of gold. Is that too much to ask?"

Was there ever such an idiot butcher, thought the Sheriff, as he nudged the Bishop in his fat ribs.

"Nay, good fellow," said he, chuckling, "I am always ready to help anyone in my shire. And since you cannot find a buyer at this price, I will buy them myself."

At this Robin began praising the Sheriff to the skies and telling him that he would not forget the kindness.

"Tut, tut," said the Sheriff, "it's nothing but a trade. Drive in your herd tomorrow to the marketplace, and you shall have money down."

"Nay, excellence," said Robin, "I cannot easily do that, for they are grazing in scattered fashion, over near Gamewell. Will you not come and choose your own beasts tomorrow?"

"Aye, that I will," said the Sheriff. "Stay with me overnight, and I will go with you in the morning."

Robin did not like the idea of staying overnight at the Sheriff's house. He had hoped to appoint a meeting place, but he now saw that this might raise doubts about him. He looked round at the company. By this time the butchers were **deep in their cups**. The Sheriff and Robin had talked in a low voice, and the lord Bishop was almost asleep.

DEEP IN THEIR CUPS
Drunk.

"Agreed," said Robin presently, and the words were no sooner out of his mouth than the door opened, and a servingman entered bearing a tray of spiced wine. At the sight of the fellow's face Robin gave a start of surprise that he instantly checked. The other also saw him, stood still a moment, and, as if forgetting something, turned about and left the hall.

It was Little John.

A dozen questions flashed across Robin's mind. What was Little John doing in the Sheriff's house? Why had he not told the band? Was he true to them? Would he betray him?

But these questions were dismissed from Robin's mind as soon as they entered. He knew that Little John was faithful and true.

Robin began foolish banter again, for the amusement of the Sheriff and his guests, all being now merry with wine.

"A song!" one of them shouted, and the cry was taken up round the table. Robin stood on his chair, and sang out:

> *"A lass and a butcher of Nottingham*
> *Agreed between them for to wed:*
> *Says he, 'I'll give ye the meat, fair dame,*
> *And ye will give me the bread.'"*

Then they joined in the chorus, pounding their cups on the tables:

> *"With a hey and a ho*
> *And a hey nonny no,*
> *A butcher of Nottingham!"*

While the song was at its height, Little John reappeared with other servants. He came up to Robin and, as if asking him if he would have more wine, said softly: "Meet me in the pantry tonight."

Robin nodded and sang loudly. The hour was

late, and presently the company broke up. The Sheriff told a servant to show Robin to his room and promised to see him at breakfast.

Robin kept his word and met Little John that night and the Sheriff the next day, but first let us turn to the story of how Little John came to be in the Sheriff's mansion.

CHAPTER 4

How Little John Entered the Sheriff's Service

"List and hearken, gentlemen,
All ye that now be here,
Of Little John, that was Knight's man,
Good mirth ye now shall hear."

I T WAS A FAIR DAY AT NOTTINGHAM, and people
crowded through all the gates. Goods of many
kinds were displayed in gaily-colored booths, and
at every street corner a free show was going on. Here and
there, stages had been erected for matches at quarterstaff, a highly popular sport.

One fellow, Eric of Lincoln, was thought to be
the finest man with the staff for miles around. His feats
were sung about in ballads through all the shire. He was

a great boaster, and today he strutted about on one of these corner stages and offered to crack any man's head for a shilling. Several had tried their skill with Eric, but he had soon sent them spinning, to the jeers of the onlookers.

A beggar sat near Eric's stage and grinned every time a head was whacked. He was a ragged fellow, dirty and unshaven. Eric caught sight of the beggar scoffing at one of his boasts and turned toward him sharply.

"How now, you dirty villain!" said he. "Mend your manners toward those who are better than you, or, **by our Lady**, I'll dust your rags for you."

The beggar still grinned. "I am always ready to mend my manners to my betters," he said, "but I am afraid you cannot teach me any better than you can dust my jacket."

BY OUR LADY
A reference to the Virgin Mary, used as a prayer or promise.

"Come up! Come up!" roared Eric, flourishing his staff.

"That I will," said the beggar, getting up with difficulty. "It will be a huge pleasure to me to take a braggart down a notch, if some good man will lend me a stout quarterstaff."

Several men offered him their staves and he took the stoutest and heaviest of all. He made a sorry figure as he climbed awkwardly upon the stage, but once there he towered a full head above Eric of Lincoln. Still, he held his stick so clumsily that the crowd laughed with glee.

Now each man looked the other up and down, watching warily for an opening. They stood so only for a moment. Eric, intent on sweeping this rash beggar speedily off the stage, attacked boldly and gave him a sounding crack on the shoulder. The beggar danced about, as though he would drop his staff from the pain, while the crowd roared. Eric raised his staff for another crushing blow. But just then the beggar came to life. Like a flash he dealt Eric a backhanded blow, such as he had never before seen. Down he went to the floor with a heavy thump, and the fickle people yelled themselves purple, for it was a new sight to see Eric of Lincoln eating dust.

But he was up again almost as soon as he had fallen, and he quickly retreated to his own ringside to gather his wits and watch for an opening.

Those who stood around now saw the merriest game of quarterstaff that was ever played inside the walls of Nottingham. Both men fenced with fine skill. Again and again Eric sought an opening under the other's guard, and just as often his blows were parried. The beggar stood sturdily beating off the attack. For a long time their blows met with steady cracks and Eric tried to be wary. But he grew mad at last and began to send down blows so fierce and fast that you would have sworn a hailstorm was pounding the roof over your head. Yet he never broke the tall beggar's guard.

Then at last the stranger changed his style of fighting. With one upward stroke he sent Eric's staff whirling through the air. With another he tapped Eric on the head, and with a third broad swing, before Eric could recover, knocked him off the stage.

People shouted and made so much ado that the shopkeepers left their stalls, and others came running from every direction. The victory of the beggar made him immensely popular. Eric had been a great bully, and many had suffered insults at his hands. So the ragged stranger found money and food and drink offered everywhere, and he feasted comfortably till the afternoon.

Then a long bow contest came on, and the beggar went to it with some of his new friends. It was held in

Little·John·overcomes·Eric·o'·Lincoln

the same arena that Robin had triumphed in, and again the Sheriff and lords and ladies graced the scene with their presences.

When the archers had stepped forward, the herald proclaimed the rules of the game: each man would shoot three shots, and he who shot best would win the prize of a team of oxen. A dozen bowmen were there, and among them some of the best fellows in the Forester's and Sheriff's companies. Down at the end of the line towered the tall beggar.

The Sheriff noted him and asked: "Who is that ragged fellow?"

"He who cracked the crown of Eric of Lincoln," was the reply.

The shooting presently began, and last of all came the beggar's turn.

"By your leave," he said loudly, "I'd like to shoot with any man here at a mark of my own placing." And he walked down the field with a slender, peeled sapling, which he stuck upright in the ground. "There," he said, "is a right good mark. Will any man try it?"

But no archer would risk his reputation on so small a target. Shortly, the beggar drew his bow with seeming carelessness and split the sapling with his arrow.

"Long live the beggar!" yelled the bystanders.

The Sheriff swore a curse and said: "This man is the best archer that I ever yet saw." He beckoned to him and asked: "Good fellow, what is your name, and where were you born?"

"In Holderness, where I was born," the man replied, "men call me Reynold Greenleaf."

"You are a sturdy fellow, Reynold Greenleaf, and deserve better apparel than that you wear. Will you enter my service? I will give you twenty marks a year, above your living, and three good suits of clothes."

"Three good suits, you say? Then I will enter your service gladly, for my back has been bare many long days."

Then Reynold turned to the crowd and shouted: "Hear ye, good people, I have entered the Sheriff's service and do not need the steers for a prize, so take them for yourselves to feast on."

At this the crowd shouted more merrily than ever and threw their caps high into the air. No one as popular as Reynold Greenleaf had come to Nottingham in many a day.

Now, you may have guessed, by this time, who Reynold Greenleaf really was: Little John.

Two days passed by. Little John insisted on eating the Sheriff's best bread and drinking his best wine. Still, the Sheriff held him in high esteem and talked of taking him along on the next hunting trip.

It was now the day of the butchers' banquet. The banquet hall was not in the main house, but connected with it by a corridor. All the servants were bustling about preparing for the feast, except Little John, who lay in bed the greater part of the day. But he presented himself at last, when the dinner was half over, and wishing to see the guests for himself, he went with the other servants to serve the wine. First, however, some of the wine passed his own lips while he went down the corridor.

When he entered the banqueting hall, whom should he see but Robin Hood himself. Imagine the surprise felt by each of these bold fellows upon seeing the other in such unexpected company. But they kept their secrets and arranged to meet each other that same night. Meanwhile, the proud Sheriff did not know that he sheltered the two chief outlaws of the whole countryside beneath his roof.

After the feast was over and the hour grew late, Little John felt faint and remembered that he had not eaten at all that day. Back he went to the pantry to see what food might be left. But there, locking up for the night, stood the fat steward.

"Good Sir Steward," said Little John, "give me food, please."

The steward looked at him grimly and rattled the keys on his belt.

"Sir Lie-a-bed," said he, "'tis late in the day to talk of eating. Since you have waited this long to be hungry, you can take your appetite back to bed again."

"Now, that I will not do," cried Little John. "Your own paunch of fat would be enough for any bear to sleep on through the winter. But my stomach wants food, and food it shall have!"

Saying this, he brushed past the steward and tried the door, but it was locked. The fat steward chuckled and jangled his keys again.

Then Little John was mad. He hammered his huge fist on the doorpanel with a blow that split an opening you could put your hand through. Little John had stooped and peered through the hole to see what food lay within reach, when the steward's keys went crack upon his crown. Then he turned on the steward and gave him such a rap that the fat fellow went rolling on the floor.

"Lie there," said Little John, "till ye find strength to go to bed. Meanwhile, I'll be about my dinner." He kicked open the pantry door and brought out a venison pie and cold roast pheasant. Placing these down on a convenient shelf, Little John ate and drank as much as he wished.

Now the Sheriff had in his kitchen a cook, a man strong and brave, who heard the noise and came in to see what had happened. There sat Little John, eating away, while the fat steward was rolled under the table like a bundle of rags.

"Is this how you ask for your supper?" said the cook, as he drew a sword that hung at his side.

"You are a foolish man to come between me and my meat," said Little John. "So defend yourself, and see that you prove the better man." And he drew his own sword and crossed weapons with the cook.

Back and forth they clashed. They fought stiffly, and neither thought of quitting. But for a full hour nei-

The·Mighty·Fight·betwixt:
Little·John·and·the·Cook:

ther could touch the other.

"I swear!" cried Little John, "you are the best swordsman that I ever yet saw. What do you say to resting and eating and drinking with me? Then we'll return to our swords."

"Agreed!" said the cook, who loved good food as well as a good fight, and they both laid down their swords and began eating heartily. The venison pie soon disappeared. Then the warriors rested a while, patted their stomachs, and smiled across at each other like best friends, for when a man has eaten he looks out pleasantly upon the world.

"And now, Reynold Greenleaf," said the cook, "we may as well settle this fight."

"True," answered Little John. "But first tell me, friend—for you are my friend from now on—what is the score we have to settle?"

"Who can handle the sword best," said the cook. "In truth, I expected to carve you up like a frying chicken by now."

"And I expected to shave your ears by now," replied Little John. "We can settle this bout in good time, but just now my master and I have need of you, and you can turn your blade to better service than that of the Sheriff."

"Whose service would that be?" asked the cook.

"Mine," answered the would-be butcher, entering the room, "and I am Robin Hood."

CHAPTER 5

How the Sheriff Lost Three Servants and Found Them Again

*"'Make good cheer,' said Robin Hood.
'Sheriff! for charity!
And for the love of Little John
Thy life is granted thee!'"*

THE COOK GASPED in amazement. Robin Hood! Under the Sheriff's very roof!

"Now, you are a brave fellow," he said. "I have heard great tales of your skill. But who might this be?"

"Men call me Little John."

"Then Little John, I like you well, on my honor as Much, the miller's son. And you, too, Robin Hood. If

56

you'll take me, I'll enter your service right gladly."

"Spoken like a brave man!" said Robin, seizing him by the hand. "But I must get back to my own bed, lest I be found here. Lucky for us, wine flowed freely in this house today, or else the noise of your combat would have brought others besides me. Now, flee the house tonight, and I will join you in the forest tomorrow."

"But, master," said the cook, "you should not stay here overnight! Come with us. The Sheriff has set a strict watch on all the gates, but I know the warden at the west gate and can get us through safely. Tomorrow you will be stopped."

"Nay, I will not," laughed Robin. "I shall go through with the Sheriff himself. Now you, Little John, and you, Much, the miller's son, go quickly. In the borders of the wood you will find my merry men. Tell them to kill two fine stags for tomorrow's supper, for we shall have great company."

And Robin left them as suddenly as he had come.

"Comrade," said Little John then, "we may as well bid the Sheriff's roof farewell. But, before we go, it seems a true pity not to take some of the Sheriff's silver plate to remember him by."

"Indeed," said the cook.

So they got a large sack and filled it with silver plate from the shelves, taken so that it would not be noticed as missing, swung the sack between them, and went into the friendly shelter of Sherwood Forest.

The next morning the servants awoke late in the Sheriff's house. The steward's cracked head was still in such a whirl that the theft went undiscovered for the time being.

Robin Hood met the Sheriff at breakfast. His host soon spoke of what was uppermost in his heart, the purchase of that fine herd of cattle near Gamewell. It was clear that a vision of them had been in his dreams. And again Robin seemed such a silly fellow that the Sheriff saw no need of hiding his thoughts, but said that he was ready to look at the herd at once.

So they set forth, Robin in his little butcher's cart, pulled by the lean mare, and the Sheriff mounted on a horse. Out of Nottingham, they took the road leading through Sherwood Forest. And as they plunged deeper among the trees, Robin whistled and sang snatches of tunes.

"Why are you so happy?" said the Sheriff. To tell the truth, the silence of the woods was making him uneasy.

"I am whistling to keep my courage up!" replied Robin.

"What is there to fear when you have the Sheriff of Nottingham beside you?" said the other.

Robin scratched his head.

"They say that Robin Hood and his men care nothing for the Sheriff," he said.

"Pooh!" said the Sheriff angrily. "I would not give that"—and he snapped his fingers—"for their lives if I could once lay hands upon them."

"But Robin Hood himself was on this very road the last time I came to town," said the other.

The Sheriff jumped at the crackling of a twig under his horse's feet and looked around.

"Did you see him?" he asked.

"Aye, that did I! He wanted the use of this mare and cart to drive to Nottingham. He said he would like to be a butcher. But look!"

As he spoke he came to a turn in the road, and before them stood a herd of the King's deer, grazing. Robin pointed to them and said:

"There is my herd of cattle, good Sheriff! How do you like them? Are they not fat?"

The Sheriff drew rein quickly. "Now, fellow," said he, "I wish I were out of this forest, for I do not care to see such herds as these or such faces as yours. Now go your own way, whoever you are, and let me go mine."

"Nay," laughed Robin, seizing the Sheriff's bridle. "I have taken too many pains to have your company to give it up so easily. Besides, I wish you to meet my friends and dine with me, since you have so lately entertained me at your table."

So saying he clapped a horn to his lips and blew three notes. The deer bounded away, there came a rustling, and out from behind cover came forty men, clad in Lincoln green and bearing bows in their hands and short swords at their sides. They ran up to Robin Hood and lifted their caps to him respectfully, while the Sheriff sat still from amazement.

"Welcome to the greenwood!" said one of the men, bending his knee in mock reverence before the Sheriff.

The Sheriff glared. It was Little John.

"Reynold Greenleaf," he said, "you have betrayed me!"

"I swear," said Little John, "that you are to blame, master. I was denied my dinner when I was at your house. But we shall set you down to a feast we hope you will enjoy."

"Well spoken, Little John," said Robin Hood. "Take his bridle, and let us honor the guest who has come to feast with us."

Then the whole company plunged into the heart of the forest.

After twisting and turning through the trees until the Sheriff's head was dizzy, the men came to an open space flanked by widespreading oaks. Under the largest of these a fire was crackling, and near it two fine stags lay ready for cooking. Around the blaze was gathered a company of yeomen quite as large as that which came with Robin Hood. They sprang up and saluted their leader.

"Good fellows!" cried Robin Hood, "while our new cook is preparing a feast worthy of our guest, let us have a few games to do him honor!"

Then while the whole glade filled with the savory smell of roasting venison, and brown pastries warmed beside the blaze, and spiced wine sent out a cordial fragrance, Robin Hood placed the Sheriff beneath the largest oak and sat down by him.

The best archers of the band set up a small pole a hundred paces away and tied a wreath to it. The archers began to shoot, and anyone who did not shoot through the garland without touching its leaves was given a good sound rap by Little John. But the shooting was expert, for the men practiced daily, and many shafts sped cleanly through the circle. Nonetheless, now and again some unlucky fellow would miss and would be sent spinning from a blow from the tall lieutenant, while the glade echoed with laughter. And a hearty guffaw even came from the Sheriff's own throat, for the spirit of Sherwood Forest was upon him.

But presently his mood was dashed. The company

sat down to eat, and the guest had two more surprises. The cook came forward to serve the food, and the Sheriff saw his own servant, whom he supposed was at that moment in the kitchen at Nottingham.

Much, the miller's son, grinned at the Sheriff's amazement and served the plates. Then the Sheriff gasped and nearly choked with rage. It was his own silverware!

"You rascals!" he sputtered. "Was it not enough to take my servants? Must you also rob me of my best silver? On my life, I will not touch your food!"

"**Grammercy!**" said Robin Hood. "The platters are only used to do your worship honor. And as for your life, for the love of Little John your life is granted you!"

So the Sheriff sat down again, and soon the cook's dishes were disappearing down his throat as rapidly as the next man's. They feasted royally and clinked each other's cups, until the sun no longer showed the pattern of the leaves upon the forest carpet.

GRAMMERCY
A word once used to express astonishment or gratitude. It comes from 'grand merci,' French words meaning great thanks.

Then the Sheriff rose and said: "I thank you, Robin Hood, once a butcher, and you, Little John, once a beggar, and you, Much, once a cook, and all you good men who have entertained me in Sherwood so well. I make no promises as to how I shall repay you when you come to Nottingham next, for I follow the King's commands. But the shadows grow long, and I must leave, if you will please show me to the road."

Then Robin Hood and all his men rose and drank the Sheriff's health, and Robin said: "If you must go at once we will not keep you—except that you have forgotten two things."

"What may they be?" asked the Sheriff, while his heart sank within him.

"You forget that you came with me today to buy a herd of cattle. And he who dines at the Greenwood Inn must pay the landlord."

The Sheriff fidgeted like a boy who has forgotten his lesson.

"I have but a small sum with me," he began apologetically.

"What is that sum?" asked Little John, "for my own wages should also come out of it!"

"And mine!" said Much.

"And mine!" smiled Robin.

The Sheriff caught his breath. "Are all these silver dishes worth anything?"

The outlaws roared at this.

"I'll tell you what, worship," said Robin, "we three rascally servants will settle our back wages for those plates. And we will keep the herd of cattle free for our own use—and the King's. But this little tavern bill should be paid! Now, what sum have you about you?"

"I have only these twenty pieces of gold, and twenty others," said the Sheriff; and it was well that he told the truth, for Robin said: "Count it, Little John."

Little John turned the Sheriff's wallet inside out.

"'Tis true enough," he said.

"Then you shall pay no more than twenty pieces for your entertainment," decreed Robin. "Is it fair, men of the greenwood?"

"Good!" echoed the others.

"The Sheriff should swear by his **patron saint** that he will not molest us," said Will Stutely.

"So be it, then," cried Little John, approaching the Sheriff. "Now, swear by your life and your patron saint."

PATRON SAINT
A saint one prays to for help and protection. St. George, who is often shown killing a dragon, is the patron saint of England.

"I swear by St. George," said the Sheriff vigorously, "that I will never disturb the outlaws in Sherwood."

But let me catch any of you out of Sherwood! he thought to himself.

Then the twenty pieces of gold were paid, and the Sheriff prepared to depart.

"I shall keep you company myself for part of the way," said Robin, "for 'twas I who brought you into the wood." And he took the Sheriff's horse by the bridle and led him through many thickets until they reached the main road.

"Now, farewell, Sheriff," said Robin, "and next time you think of cheating a poor man, remember the cattle you tried to buy at Gamewell."

So saying he slapped the horse's rear, and off went the Sheriff on the road to Nottingham.

CHAPTER 6

How Robin Hood Met Will Scarlet

"The youngster was clothed in scarlet red,
In scarlet fine and gay;
And he did frisk it o'er the plain,
*And chanted a **roundelay**."*

O NE FINE MORNING soon after the proud Sheriff had been humbled, Robin Hood and Little John passed not far from the footbridge where they had fought their memorable battle and directed their steps to the brook to quench their thirst.

On each side of the dusty highway stretched out broad fields of tender young wheat. On the far side of the fields rose the sturdy oaks and beeches and ashes of the forest. At

ROUNDELAY
A simple song with a line that repeats often.

67

their feet violets peeped out shyly and greeted them with a fragrance that made their hearts glad. Once they reached the bank of the brook, the two friends lay flat on their backs amid some clover blossoms and gazed up at the clouds in silence.

Presently they heard someone coming up the road whistling gaily, as though he owned the whole world and it was made only to whistle in.

"Here comes a cheery bird!" said Robin, raising up on his elbow. "Let us lie still and hope that his purse is not as light as his heart."

So they lay still, and soon up came a stranger dressed in scarlet and silk and wearing a jaunty hat with a curling feather in it. His whole costume was scarlet, from the feather to the silk **hose** on his legs. A good sword hung at his side, its scabbard all embossed with tilting knights and weeping ladies. His hair was long and yellow and hung in clusters about his shoulders.

HOSE
Close-fitting leg-gings, like stock-ings, that attached at the waist to a jacket.

Little John clucked at this sight but then added: "Not so bad a build for all his prettiness," he said. "Look, those legs are strong and straight. His arms hang from full shoulders. I promise you he can use his sword right well."

"Nay," answered Robin. "He is nothing but a ladies' man from court. I'll bet my long bow against a shilling that he would run at the sight of a quarterstaff. Stay behind this bush, and I will get some sport out of him. His silk purse may hold more pennies than the law allows to one man in Sherwood."

So saying, Robin Hood stepped out and planted himself in the way of the scarlet stranger. The latter, seeing Robin, neither slowed nor quickened his pace but sauntered straight ahead, looking to the right and left, but never once at Robin.

"Stop!" said the outlaw. "What do you mean by running over a wayfarer?"

"Why should I stop, good fellow?" said the stranger in a smooth voice, looking at Robin for the first time.

"Because I ask you to," replied Robin.

"And who may you be?" asked the other coolly.

"My name does not matter," said Robin, "but I am a public tax gatherer. If your purse has more than a just number of shillings, I must lighten it some, for there are many worthy people around here who have less than the just amount. Therefore, kind sir, hand over your purse, that I may judge its weight."

Merry·Robin·stops·a·Stranger·
in·Scarlet :·

The scarlet stranger smiled sweetly, as though a lady were paying him a compliment.

"Your speech amuses me greatly," he said calmly. "Pray continue, if you are not done, for I am in no hurry this morning."

"I have said all that is needed," retorted Robin, beginning to grow red. "Nonetheless, I have other arguments that may not be so pleasing to your dainty skin. Stand and deliver. I promise to deal fairly with your purse."

"Alas!" said the stranger, with a little shrug of his shoulders. "I am deeply sorry that I cannot show my purse to every rogue who asks to see it. But I really could not. I need every penny it contains. Pray, stand aside."

"Nay, I will not! And it will go harder with you if you do not yield at once."

"Good fellow," said the other gently, "have I not listened to you with patience? Now, that is all I promised to do. My conscience is clear, and I must go on my way."

"Hold, I say!" said Robin hotly, for he knew Little John must be chuckling at this from behind the bushes. "Or else I shall bloody those fair locks of yours!" And he swung his quarterstaff threateningly.

"Alas!" moaned the stranger, shaking his head.

"Now I shall have to run this fellow through with my sword! And I had hoped to be a peaceable man from now on!" And sighing deeply he drew his shining blade.

"Put away your weapon," said Robin. "'Tis too pretty a piece of steel to get cracked with a common oak cudgel—and that is what would happen on the first pass I made at you. Get a stick like mine out of the undergrowth, and we will fight fairly, man to man."

The stranger thought a moment and eyed Robin from head to foot. Then he unbuckled his scabbard, laid it and the sword aside, and walked deliberately over to the oak thicket. Choosing from among the saplings, he found a stout little tree to his liking. He laid hold of it, without stopping to cut it, and gave a tug. Up it came, root and all, as though it were a stalk of corn, and the stranger walked back, trimming it quietly, as if pulling up trees were the easiest thing in the world.

From his hiding place, Little John saw the feat. "By our Lady," he muttered to himself, "I'm glad not be in Master Robin's boots!"

Whatever Robin thought upon seeing the stranger's strength, he did not utter a word nor budge an inch.

Then back and forth the fighters swayed, their

cudgels pounding, knocking off splinters and bark, and threatening to break bone, muscle and skin. Back and forth they pranced, kicking up a cloud of dust, and gasping for fresh air. Three times Robin struck the scarlet man with blows that would have bowled over an ordinary man. Only twice did the scarlet man hit Robin, but the second blow was enough to finish him. The first had been delivered over the knuckles, and though it was a glancing stroke, it almost broke Robin's fingers, so that he could not easily raise his staff again. And while he was dancing about in pain, the other's staff came swinging through the dust cloud—zip!—and struck him under the arm. Down went Robin as though he were a bowling pin—flat down into the dust of the road. But despite the pain, he was getting up again to fight on, when Little John interfered.

"Hold!" said he, bursting out of the bushes and seizing the stranger's weapons. "Hold, I say!"

"I would not strike him while he was down," answered the stranger quietly. "But if there is a nest of you hatching here, cluck out the other chicks, and I'll fight them all."

"Not for all the deer in Sherwood!" cried Robin.

"I'll fight you no more, for I feel truly sore in wrist and body. Nor shall any of mine molest you."

In fact, Robin did not look good. His clothes were coated with dirt, one of his hose had slipped half way down from his knee, the sleeve of his **jerkin** was split, and his face was streaked with sweat and dirt. Little John eyed him with amusement.

"Now, good master," said he, "the sport you kicked up has left you in a sorry state. Let me dust your coat for you."

JERKIN
A leather vest that covered the hips.

"It has been dusted enough already," replied Robin. "And I now believe the Scripture saying that all men are made of dust, for it has sifted me through and through and lined my throat an inch deep." And he went to the brook, drank deep, and washed his face and hands.

All this time the stranger had been eyeing Robin attentively and listening to his voice, as though striving to recall it.

"If I'm not mistaken," he said at last, "you are the famous outlaw Robin Hood."

"You are right," replied Robin. "But my fame has tumbled sadly about in the dust today."

"Now, why did I not know you at once?" continued the stranger. "This battle did not need to happen, for I came to find you today and thought I could remember your face and voice. Do you not know me, Rob? Have you ever been to Gamewell Lodge?"

"Will Gamewell! My dear cousin Will Gamewell!" shouted Robin, throwing his arms about Will with affection. "What a clod I was not to recognize you! But it has been years since we parted, and your schooling has polished you up greatly."

Will embraced his cousin no less happily. "We are equal on not knowing our relatives," he said, "for you have changed and strengthened much from the boy I used to run races with in old Sherwood."

"But why do you seek me?" asked Robin. "You know I am an outlaw and dangerous company. How is my uncle? And have you heard of Maid Marian lately?"

"Your last question first," answered Will, laughing. "I saw Maid Marian not long after the great shooting match at Nottingham, when you won her the golden arrow. She prizes it among her dearest possessions, though it has made her an enemy of the Sheriff's proud daughter. Maid Marian asked me to tell you, if I ever saw you, that she must return to Queen Eleanor's court, but she can never forget the happy days in Sherwood. As for the old Squire, he is still strong and hearty. He speaks of you as a sad young dog, but is secretly proud of your skill with the bow and of the way you are pestering the Sheriff.

" 'Twas for my father's sake that I am now an outlaw like yourself. He had a steward, a surly fellow, who, while I was away at school, bootlicked his way into favor until he lorded it over the whole house. Then he grew right saucy and defiant, but my father ignored it. He thought the fellow indispensable in managing the estate. When I came back it irked me to see the fellow strut about as though he owned the place. He was sly enough with me at first and would browbeat the Squire only while I was out of earshot. It happened one day, however, that I heard loud voices through an open window and paused to listen. That wicked servant called my father 'a meddling old fool.' 'You are a fool and meddler yourself,' I shouted, springing through the window. 'Take that for your impudence!' And I struck him a heavier blow than I intended, for I have some strength in mine arm. The fellow rolled over and never breathed again. I think I broke his neck. I knew that the Sheriff would use this as a reason to hound my father if I stayed, so I told him I would seek you in Sherwood."

"For a man escaping the law you took it about as coolly as one could wish," said Robin Hood. "To see you come along decked out in all your plumage, one would think you had not a care in all the world. Indeed, I remarked to Little John here that I hoped your purse was not as light as your heart."

"Perhaps you meant head," laughed Will. "And is this Little John? Shake hands with me, if you will, and promise me to cross a staff with me in friendly bout some day!"

"That will I!" said Little John heartily. "Here's my hand on it. What is your last name again?"

"'Tis to be changed," interjected Robin, "to confuse the men looking for him. Ah! I have it! In scarlet he came to us, and that shall be his name. Welcome to Sherwood, Will Scarlet!"

"Aye, welcome, Will Scarlet!" said Little John, and they all clasped hands again and swore to be true each to the other.

CHAPTER 7

How Robin Hood Met Friar Tuck

"The friar took Robin Hood on his back,
Deep water he did bestride,
And spoke neither good word nor bad,
Till he came at the other side."

IT HAD BEEN ROBIN HOOD'S custom to pick out the best men in all the countryside. Whenever he heard of someone noted for skill in any feat of arms he would seek the man and test him in a personal encounter—which did not always end happily for Robin. And when he had found a man to his liking, he offered him a place with his band of outlaws.

Thus it came about that one day after archery practice, in which Little John struck down a stag five hundred feet away, Robin Hood began to boast.

"I would travel an hundred miles to find one who could match you!" he cried, clapping the burly fellow on the shoulder.

At this Will Scarlet laughed roundly.

"There's a friar living in Fountain's Abbey—Tuck, by name—who can beat both him and you," he said.

Robin pricked up his ears.

"By our Lady," he said, "I'll neither eat nor drink till I see this friar."

He set about arming himself for the adventure at once. On his head he placed a cap of steel, underneath his Lincoln green he wore a coat of **chain mail**, and with a sword and **buckler** strapped at his side he made a good show. He also took with him his bow and a sheaf of arrows.

CHAIN MAIL
Flexible armor made of small interlocked metal rings that offered protection from arrows and swords.

BUCKLER
A small round shield held at arm's length by a handle.

He pressed forward by winding ways till he came to a green, broad pastureland, at whose edge flowed a stream with willows and rushes on the banks. It flowed calmly, as though it had some depth in the middle. Robin did not fancy getting his feet wet or his fine suit of chain mail rusted, so he paused on the bank to rest and take his bearings.

As he sat quietly under the shade of a drooping willow he heard snatches of a merry song from the other side, then the sound of two men's voices arguing. One was describing the merits of **hasty pudding**, and the other strongly preferred meat pie, "especially," said this one, "when flavored with young onions!"

"Grammercy!" muttered Robin to himself, "that is a **tantalizing** speech to a hungry man!"

But in truth the voices seemed curiously alike.

HASTY PUDDING
Boiled oatmeal; porridge.

TANTALIZING
In Greek mythology, Tantalus was a king who was favored by the gods and invited to their feasts. He betrayed their secrets to humans and roasted his own son to feed to them in order to test their divine knowledge. As punishment, he was tortured with eternal hunger and thirst. He was sent to the underworld and stood in water up to his neck. If he tried to drink, the water sank away. A branch of fruit hung above him and if he tried to reach it, wind lifted the branch away. The word tantalize comes from his name and means to tempt.

Presently the willows parted on the other bank, and Robin could hardly resist laughing outright. The mystery was explained. It was not two men who had done all this singing and talking, but one—a fat friar sitting by the water's edge who wore a long cloak

over his round frame, tied with a cord in the middle. On his head was a knight's helmet, and in his hand was a huge meat pie.

First the friar took off his helmet. His head was as round as an apple. A fringe of short, curling black hair grew round the base of his skull, but the crown of his head was as bare and shiny as an egg. His cheeks also were smooth, red and shiny, and his little grey eyes danced about with the funniest air imaginable. Good humor and fat living stood out all over him, yet for all that he looked able to take care of himself with any man. His short neck was thick like that of a bull, his shoulders were set far back, and his arms sprouted from them like two oak limbs. As he sat down the cloak fell open, revealing a sword and buckler like Robin's.

Robin's heart fell within him when he saw the meat pie, which was about to be devoured before his very eyes. The friar lost no time in thrusting one hand deep into the pie, while he **crossed himself** with the other.

Thereupon Robin seized his bow and fitted a shaft.

CROSSED HIMSELF
A gesture, called the sign of the cross, made by Roman Catholic, Eastern Orthodox and Anglican Christians. One traces the form of a cross between the forehead, chest and shoulders to remember Jesus's death on the cross and to ask for God's blessing.

"Hey, friar!" he sang out, "carry me over the water, or else I cannot answer for your safety."

The friar was startled by the unexpected greeting and laid his hand upon his sword. Then he saw Robin's arrow pointing at him.

"Put down your bow, fellow," he shouted back, "and I will bring you over the brook. It is our duty in life to help each other, and your arrow shows me that you are a man worthy of attention."

So the friar got up gravely, though his eyes twinkled with a cunning light, laid aside his pie and his cloak and his sword and his buckler, and waded across the stream with waddling dignity. Then he took Robin Hood upon his back and spoke neither good word nor bad till he came to the other side.

Robin leaped lightly off his back and said: "I am much beholden to you, good father."

"Beholden, you say!" answered the friar, drawing his sword, "then, by my faith, you shall repay your debt. Now, my own affairs, which are of a spiritual kind, and much more important than yours, lie on the other side of the stream. You seem to be a man who would not refuse to serve the church. Therefore, I pray of you that, what-

The·Merry·Friar·carrieth·
Robin·across·the·Water:·

ever I have done for you, you will also do for me. In short, you must carry me back again."

This was said courteously enough, but so suddenly had the friar drawn his sword that Robin had no time to unsling his bow from his back (where he had placed it to avoid getting it wet) or to unfasten his sword, so he stalled.

"But, father, I shall get my feet wet."

"Are your feet any better than mine?" said the other. "I fear that I am already so wet that I shall get **rheumatic pains** as a penance."

"I am not as strong as you," continued Robin. "That sword and buckler would be my undoing on the uncertain footing in the stream, to say nothing of your holy flesh and bones."

RHEUMATIC PAINS
Pain caused by swelling in the muscles or joints.

"Then I will lighten up, somewhat," replied the friar calmly. "Promise to carry me across and I will lay aside my war gear."

"Agreed," said Robin, and he took him up as he had promised.

Now, the stones at the bottom of the stream were round and slippery, and the current swept along strongly, waist-deep in the middle. Robin had a heavier load than the friar had carried, and he did not know the ford, so he went stumbling along, stepping into a deep hole, stumbling over a boulder, and nearly plunging them both into the current. But the fat friar hung on and dug his heels into Robin's ribs as if he were riding in a tournament. Sweat ran down Robin, and he gasped like the winded man he was. But at last he managed to stagger out onto the bank.

No sooner had he set the friar down than Robin seized his own sword.

"Now, holy friar," said he, panting, "what do the Scriptures say? 'Be not weary of doing good.' You must carry me back again, or I swear that I will make a **cheesecloth** out of your jacket!"

The friar's grey eyes once more twinkled with a gleam that boded no good to Robin, but his voice was as calm and courteous as ever.

CHEESE-CLOTH
Cloth so loosely woven that liquids easily drain through it in making cheese.

"Your wits are keen, my son," he said, "and the waters of the stream have not quenched your spirit. Once more will I bend my back and carry the weight of the haughty."

So Robin mounted again in glee and carried his
sword in his hand. But while he was thinking of what he
would say when he arrived on the other side, he felt himself slipping from the friar's back. He clutched frantical-
ly to save himself, but the surface was too round to grasp
and he was hampered by his weapon, so down he went
with a loud splash into the middle of the stream, where
the crafty friar had carried him.

"There!" said the holy man. "You choose, my fine
fellow, whether you will sink or swim!" And he reached
his own bank without more ado, while Robin thrashed
about until he managed to grasp a willow branch and
haul himself ashore on the opposite side.

Robin's rage was furious. He took his bow and
his arrows and let fly one shaft after another at the friar.
But they rattled harmlessly off his steel buckler, while he
laughed as if they were hailstones.

"Shoot on, shoot on!" he sang out.

So Robin shot until all his arrows were gone.

"You villain!" he shouted. "Come within reach of
my sword and, friar or not, I'll shave you closer than a
bald monk was ever shaved before!"

"Soft!" said the friar calmly. "Hard words are

cheap, and you may need your wind presently. If you would like a bout with swords, meet me half way in the stream."

And the friar waded into the brook, sword in hand, where he was met half way by the hotheaded outlaw.

Then began a fierce battle. Up and down, in and out, back and forth they fought. The swords flashed in the rays of the declining sun and then met with a clash that would have shivered less sturdy weapons or disarmed less sturdy men. Many blows were landed, but each man wore an undercoat of linked mail that could not be pierced. Nonetheless, their ribs ached at the force of the blows. Twice they paused, caught their breath, and looked hard each at the other. Never before had either met so strong a fellow.

Finally, during a furious exchange, Robin stepped on a rolling stone and went down on his knees. But the friar would not take this advantage. He paused until Robin could get up.

"Now, by our Lady," cried the outlaw, using his favorite expression, "you are the best swordsman I've met in many a long day. I beg a favor of you."

"What is it?" said the other.

"Allow me to blow three blasts on my horn."

"Blow till your breath fails," said the friar.

Then Robin Hood blew three blasts, and fifty men came racing over the hillside.

"Whose men are these?" said the friar.

"Mine," said Robin Hood, feeling that his time to laugh had come at last.

Then the friar said in his turn: "And will you grant me a favor like I gave to you? Allow me to whistle three times."

"That I will do," said Robin, "or else I lack courtesy."

The friar put the horn to shame by the piercing whistles he blew; fifty powerful dogs came running and jumping so swiftly that they reached their bank as soon as Robin Hood's men had reached his side.

Then Stutely, Much, Little John, and the other outlaws sent arrows whizzing towards the opposite bank, but the dogs, well-trained by the friar, dodged the missiles cleverly and fetched them back again in their mouths, just as dogs catch sticks.

"I've never seen the like of this in all my days!" cried Little John, amazed. "It's witchcraft."

"Take off your dogs, Friar Tuck!" shouted Will Scarlet, who had just then run up and now stood laughing heartily at the scene.

"Friar Tuck!" exclaimed Robin, astounded. "Are you Friar Tuck? Then am I your friend, for you are the man I came to find."

"I am but a poor **anchorite**," he said, whistling to his pack, "called Friar Tuck of Fountain's Dale. For seven years have I tended the Abbey here, preached on Sundays, married and christened and buried folk, and fought too, if it were needed. And, if it does not smack too much of boasting, I have not yet met the man that I would yield to. But I would like to know who you are."

ANCHORITE
Someone who lives alone as a hermit, usually for religious reasons.

"Robin Hood, the outlaw, has been assisting you at this christening," said Will Scarlet, glancing at the two men's dripping garments. And the whole band burst into a shout of laughter, in which Robin and Friar Tuck joined.

"Robin Hood!" cried the good friar, holding his sides; "are you indeed that famous yeoman? Then I like you well, and had I known you earlier I would have both carried you across and shared my pasty pie with you."

"To speak truly," replied Robin gaily, "'twas that same pie that led me to be rude. Now bring it and your dogs and go with us to Sherwood Forest. We have need of you. We will build you a hermitage, and you shall keep us from evil ways. Will you join our band?"

"That I will!" cried Friar Tuck.

CHAPTER 8

How Allan-a-Dale's Courting Was Aided

*"'What is thy name?' then said Robin Hood,
'Come tell me, without any fail.'
'By the faith o' my body,' then said the young man,
'My name 'tis Allan-a-Dale.'"*

F
RIAR TUCK AND MUCH, the miller's son, became
good friends over the steaming stew they cooked
together for the merry men that evening. Tuck
was mightily pleased when he found a man in the forest
who cooked so well, while Much marvelled at the friar's
knowledge of herbs and woodland things that flavored a
stew greatly. So they gabbed together like two old gossips
and, between them, made such a tasty meal that Robin
Hood and his followers seemed as if they would never

stop eating. And the friar said grace, too, over the food, and Robin said "Amen!" And from then on they always had **Mass** on Sundays.

MASS
The religious service of the Roman Catholic Church.

Robin walked in the wood that evening with his stomach full and his heart, therefore, full of love for other men.

He did not stop the first passerby, as he often did. Instead he stepped behind a tree when he heard a man's voice singing and waited.

Like Will Scarlet, this fellow was clad in scarlet, though he did not look quite as fine a gentleman. He was a sturdy yeoman of honest face, with a voice far sweeter than Will's. He seemed to be a strolling **minstrel**. He carried a harp in his hand, which he strummed, while his tenor voice rang out with:

MINSTREL
Minstrels were traveling singers and poets who usually also played the harp.

> *"Hey down, a down, a down!*
> *I've a lassie back in town;*
> *Come day, come night,*
> *Come dark or light,*
> *She will wed me, back in town!"*

Robin let the singer pass.

"'Tis not in me to disturb a lover this night," he muttered, as a memory of Marian came back to him. "May their wedding be a happy one."

So Robin went back to his camp, where he told of the minstrel.

"If any of you set eyes on him after this," he said finally, "bring him to me, for I wish to talk with him."

The very next day his wish was answered. Little John and Much, the miller's son, were out together on a hunting expedition when they spied the same young man—at least they thought it must be he, for he was clad in scarlet and carried a harp in his hand. But now he came drooping along, his clothes all in tatters, and at every step he sighed. Little John and Much stepped forward.

No sooner did the young man catch sight of them than he bent his bow and held an arrow back to his ear.

"Stand off!" he said. "What do you want with me?"

"Put down your weapon," said Much; "we will not harm you, but you must come before our master, under his oak tree."

So the minstrel put down his bow and allowed himself to be led to Robin Hood.

"How, now!" said Robin, when he saw the minstrel's sorry look. "Are you not the one I heard yesterday singing so cheerfully about 'a lassie back i' the town'?"

"The same in body, sir," replied the other sadly, "but my spirit is sadly changed."

"Tell me your tale," said Robin; "perhaps I can help you."

"No man on earth can do that, I fear," said the stranger, "but I'll tell you the tale. Yesterday I stood pledged to a maid and thought I would marry her soon. But she has been taken from me and is to become an old knight's bride this very day. As for me, I do not care what happens to me, or how soon, without her."

"Be brave!" said Robin. "How did the old knight get this sudden advantage?"

"This way: the **Normans** overrun us, and no one can oppose them. This old Crusader coveted the land where my lady dwells. The estate is not large, but it is all her own. Knowing this, her brother says she must marry a

NORMANS
People of Scandinavian descent who occupied Normandy, a region of France, in the 10th century. England was conquered by the Normans in 1066.

nobleman who has a title, and he and the old knight
have fixed it up for today."

"But surely," began Robin.

"Hear me out, sir," said the minstrel. "Perhaps
you think me a sorry dog not to make fight of this. But
the old knight cannot be reached. I threw one
of his **varlets** into a thorn hedge, and another
into a water barrel, and a third head-first into
a ditch. But I couldn't do any fighting at all."

VARLET
A servant of bad character.

"Does the maid love you?" asked Robin.

"She says she loves me right well," said the minstrel. "I have a little ring of hers which I have kept for
seven long years."

"What is your name?" said Robin then.

"Allan-a-Dale," replied the young man.

"What will you give me, Allan-a-Dale," said
Robin Hood, "in ready gold, to deliver your true love to
you again?"

"I have only five shillings," said Allan. "But are
you not Robin Hood?"

Robin nodded.

"Then you, if anyone, can aid me!" said Allan-a-
Dale eagerly. "And if you give me back my love, I swear I

will serve you truly forever."

"Where is this wedding to take place, and when?" asked Robin.

"At Plympton Church, scarcely five miles from here, at three o'clock in the afternoon."

"Then to Plympton we will go!" cried Robin, suddenly springing into action. He gave out orders like a general: "Will Stutely, have twenty-four men over at Plympton Church at three this afternoon. Much, cook up some porridge for this youth! Will Scarlet, you will see to dressing him for his wedding. And Friar Tuck, be ready, good book in hand, at the church—perhaps you had better go ahead of us all."

THE FAT BISHOP OF HEREFORD was full of pomp that day at Plympton Church. He was to celebrate the marriage of old Sir Stephen—a returned Crusader—and a young woman. All the gentry in the vicinity were to attend. The church itself was gaily decorated with flowers for the ceremony, while out in the churchyard at one side brown ale flowed freely for all the servants.

The guests were beginning to assemble, when the Bishop saw a minstrel clad in green walk up boldly to the door and peer in. It was Robin Hood, who had borrowed Allan's harp.

"Who are you, fellow," said the Bishop, "and what do you want here?"

"May it please your reverence," returned Robin, bowing very humbly, "I am but a strolling musician, called the best in the whole North Country, and I hope my strumming might add pleasure to the wedding today."

"What tune can you play?" demanded the Bishop.

"I can play a tune so merry that a sad lover will forget he is jilted," said Robin. "I can play another tune that will make a bride leave her lord at the altar. I can play another tune that will bring loving souls together even though they were five miles away from each other."

"Then welcome, minstrel," said the Bishop. "Music pleases me right well, and if you can play up to your talk, it will indeed grace our ceremony. Let us have a sample of your playing."

"Nay, I must not pluck string until the bride and groom have come."

"As you will," said the Bishop.

Then up the lane to the church came the old knight slowly, leaning on a cane, followed by ten archers outfitted in scarlet and gold.

After them came a sweet lass, leaning on her brother's arm. Her hair was like glistering gold, and her eyes were like blue violets that peep out shyly at the sun. Her complexion had the tinting of a seashell, and her face was flushed as though she had been crying. But she walked with a proud air, as though she defied the world to crush her spirit. She had two maids with her. One held the bride's gown off the ground, the other carried flowers.

"Now, by all the wedding bells that ever were rung," said Robin boldly, "this is the worst-matched pair that my eyes ever beheld!"

"Silence!" said a man who stood near.

The Bishop had hurriedly donned his gown and stood ready to meet the couple.

But Robin paid no attention to him. He let the knight and his ten archers pass by, then he walked up to the bride.

"Courage, lady!" he whispered, "there is another minstrel near who may play more to your liking."

Robin·Hood·Aeps·betwixt·
Sir·Stephen·and·his·Bride:

The lady glanced at him with a frightened look but read such honesty and kindness in his glance that she brightened and gave him a grateful look.

"Stand aside, fool!" cried her brother angrily.

"Nay, I bring good fortune to the bride," said Robin, laughing.

And he was allowed to walk by her side up to the altar.

"Now strike up your music, fellow!" ordered the Bishop.

"Right gladly," said Robin, "if you will let me choose my instrument, for sometimes I like the harp, and other times I think the horn makes the merriest music in all the world."

And he drew his bugle from underneath his green cloak and blew three notes that made the church rafters ring.

"Seize him!" yelled the Bishop. "These are Robin Hood's tricks!"

The ten archers rushed forward from the rear of the church, where they had been stationed. But they were blocked by the onlookers, who rose from their pews in alarm and crowded the aisles. Meanwhile Robin leaped lightly over the altar rail and stationed himself in a nook by the altar.

"Stand where you are!" he shouted, drawing his bow. "The first man to pass the rail dies. And all you who have come to witness a wedding stay in your seats. We shall have one, but the bride shall choose her own groom!"

Then there was another great commotion at the door, and Robin's men came marching in, with Will Stutely at their head. They seized the ten archers and the bride's scowling brother and bound them as prisoners.

Then in came Allan-a-Dale with Will Scarlet for his best man. And they walked solemnly down the aisle and stood at the altar.

"Before a maiden weds, she chooses," said Robin. "Now, maiden, whom will you have as your husband?"

She answered not in words but smiled with a glad light in her eyes, walked over to Allan, and clasped her arms about his neck.

"That is her true love," said Robin. "And the true lovers shall be married at this time. Now, my lord Bishop, proceed with the ceremony!"

"That shall not be," protested the Bishop. "The **banns** must be cried three times in the church—such is the law of our land."

"Come here, Little John," called Robin impatiently, and he pulled off the bishop's frock from his back and put it on Little John.

BANNS
An announcement in church of a proposed marriage, usually made weekly for three weeks.

"You're the finest bishop that ever I saw in my life," said Robin. "Now, cry the banns."

So Little John climbed awkwardly into the choir and he called the banns for the marriage of the maid and Allan-a-Dale once, twice, and thrice.

"Good enough!" said Robin. "Now, I see a worthy friar in the back of this church who can say a better service than my lord Bishop of Hereford. My lord Bishop shall be a witness and seal the papers, but you, good friar, bless this pair with your book and candle."

So Friar Tuck, who had been back in one corner of the church all along, came forward. Allan and his maid kneeled before him, while the old knight, held unwilling as a witness, gnashed his teeth in helpless rage. The friar began the ceremony.

When he asked: "Who gives this woman?" Robin stepped up and answered in a clear voice: "I do! I, Robin Hood of Sherwood! And anyone who takes her from Allan-a-Dale shall pay dearly."

And so the two were declared man and wife.

How Robin Hood Fought Guy of Gisborne

"'I dwell by dale and down,' said he,
'And Robin to take I'm sworn;
And when I am called by my right name,
I am Guy of good Gisborne.'"

R OBIN HOOD'S NAME and deeds had reached the King's ears in London, and he sent word to the Sheriff to capture the outlaw, or lose his office. So the Sheriff tried to surprise Robin Hood in the forest, but always without success. He also increased the price put on Robin's head, in the hope that the best men of the kingdom would try to capture him.

There was a certain Guy of Gisborne, a hired knight of the King's army, who heard of Robin and of the price on his head. Sir Guy was one of the best men with a bow or sword in all the King's service, but his heart was black and treacherous. He obtained the King's permission to hunt down the outlaw and he came to the Sheriff at Nottingham.

"I have come to capture Robin Hood," said he, "and mean to have him, dead or alive."

"I will aid you gladly," answered the Sheriff. "How many men do you need?"

"None," replied Sir Guy. "I must go alone. But you hold your men in readiness at Barnesdale, and when you hear a blast from this silver bugle, come quickly, for I shall have the sly Robin within my clutches."

"It shall be done," said the Sheriff. And he gave such orders, and Guy of Gisborne left Nottingham in disguise.

NOW AS IT HAPPENED, Robin Hood and Little John had come near having a quarrel that morning because both had seen a curious-looking fellow, and each wanted to challenge him alone. But Robin would not give way to his lieutenant and approached the curious-looking stranger himself.

ROBIN·and·LITTLE·JOHN· go· their·ways· in· search· of· Adventure:

He seemed to be a three-legged creature at first sight, but on coming nearer Robin saw that it was really nothing but a poorly-clad man, who had covered up his rags with the sun-dried skin of a horse, complete with the head, tail, and mane. The skin of the head made a helmet, while the tail gave the odd three-legged appearance.

"Good morning," said Robin cheerily, "by the bow you bear in your hand, I reckon that you should be a good archer."

"Fairly good," said the stranger. "But it's not archery that I am thinking of this morning. I have lost my way."

I could have believed it was your wits you'd lost! thought Robin, smiling. Then aloud he said, "I'll lead you through the woods, and you will tell me your business."

"Who are you to ask me my business?" asked the other roughly. "I am one of the King's Rangers," replied Robin, "set here to guard his deer."

"Since you are a Ranger, I must demand your service," returned the stranger. "I am on the King's business and seek an outlaw called Robin Hood. Are you one of his men?" eyeing him keenly.

"Nay, God forbid!" said Robin. "But what want you with him?"

"That is another tale. But I'd rather meet with that proud outlaw than forty pounds of the King's money."

Robin now understood the stranger's intentions.

"Come with me, good sir," said he, "and perhaps a little later in the day I can show you Robin's hideaways. Meanwhile let us try our mastery at shooting arrows."

The other agreed, and they cut down two willow branches and set them up at a distance of sixty yards.

"The first shot to you," said Robin.

"No," said the other, "I will follow you."

So Robin stepped forward and carelessly sent his shaft whizzing toward the wand, missing it by just an inch. The stranger in the horsehide followed with more care, yet missed by a wider margin.

On the second round the stranger led off and landed neatly within the small garland at the top of the target, but Robin shot far better and split the branch itself clean down the middle.

"A blessing on you!" shouted Horsehide. "I never saw such shooting as that! You may be better than Robin Hood himself. But you have not yet told me your name."

"I must keep it secret till you have told me your own," said Robin.

"I am proud to tell it," said the other. "I am sworn to take bold Robin and I would tell him to his face, if he were not so great a coward. I am Guy of Gisborne."

He said this with a great show of pride, and he strutted back and forth, forgetful that he had just been beaten at archery.

Robin eyed him quietly. "I think I have heard of you elsewhere. Do you not bring men to the gallows for a living?"

"Aye, but only outlaws such as Robin Hood."

"But what harm has Robin Hood done you?"

"He is a highway robber," said Sir Guy, evading the question.

"Has he ever taken anything from the rich that he did not give again to the poor? Does he not protect the women and children and side with the weak and helpless? Is not his greatest crime shooting a few of the King's deer?"

"Enough of your questions," said Sir Guy impatiently. "I suspect more than ever that you are one of Robin's men yourself."

"I have told you I am not," said Robin briefly. "But if I am to help you catch him, what is your plan?"

"Do you see this silver bugle?" said the other. "A long blast upon it will summon the Sheriff and all his men once I have Robin within my grasp. And if you show him to me I'll give you half of my forty-pound reward."

"I would not help hang a man for ten times forty pounds," said the outlaw. "Yet will I point out Robin to you for the reward I find at my sword's point. I myself am Robin Hood."

"Then have at you!" cried the other, springing swiftly into action. His sword came from beneath the

horse's hide with the speed that comes from long practice, and before Robin had chance to guard himself, Sir
Guy slashed at him. Robin dodged the lunge and drew
his own weapon.

"A foul trick!" said he grimly, "to strike at a man
who is unprepared."

Then neither spoke more but fell to work sternly—lunge and thrust and **parry**. For two full
hours the weapons struck together, and neither Robin Hood nor Sir Guy would yield an
inch. The fighters glared at each other, the fires
of hatred burning in their eyes. One was fighting for his
life, the other for a reward and the King's favor.

PARRY
To ward off a
weapon or
a blow.

Still the gleaming blades circled swiftly in the
peaceful sunlight and hissed like maddened serpents.
Neither had yet touched the other, until Robin unluckily
stumbled over the root of a tree, and Sir Guy, instead of
giving him the chance to recover himself, as any true
knight would have done, struck Robin while he was
down and wounded him in the left side.

"Ah, dear Lady in Heaven," gasped Robin, utter-
ing his favorite prayer, "shield me now! 'Twas never a
man's destiny to die before his day."

And he sprang up again and came straight at Sir Guy with an unexpected stroke. The knight had raised his weapon high to give a final blow, when Robin reached beneath his guard. One swift lunge, and Sir Guy of Gisborne staggered backward with a deep groan, Robin's sword through his throat.

Robin looked at the slain man regretfully.

"You did bring it upon yourself," said he; "I would not willingly have killed you."

He looked at his own wound. It was not serious, so he soon staunched the blood and bound up the cut. Then he dragged the dead body into the bushes, took off the horse's hide, and put it upon himself. He placed his own cloak upon Sir Guy and marked his face so no one might tell who had been slain. Robin's figure was not too much different from Sir Guy's.

Pulling the horsehide well over himself, so that the helmet hid most of his face, Robin seized the silver bugle and blew a long blast.

In twenty-five minutes a **score** of the Sheriff's best archers came running up.

"Did you signal us?" they asked, approaching Robin.

SCORE
Twenty.

Robin Hood slayeth Guy of Gisbourne.

"Aye," said he, going to meet the puffing Sheriff.

"What news, Sir Guy?" said the Sheriff.

"Robin Hood and Guy of Gisborne had a fight, and he that wears Robin's cloak lies yonder."

"The best news I have heard in all my life!" exclaimed the Sheriff, rubbing his hands. "I wish that we could have saved him for hanging—though I cannot now complain."

"But I see you have not escaped without a scratch," continued the Sheriff, becoming talkative through pure glee. "Here, one of you men! Give Sir Guy of Gisborne your horse. You others bury that dog of an outlaw where he lies, and let us hasten back to Nottingham."

So they put spurs to their horses, and as they rode, Robin forced himself to talk merrily.

"A favor, Sheriff?" he asked as they reached the gates of the town.

"What is it, sir? You have only to ask," said the Sheriff. "You can ask for double your reward, and it will be yours. It isn't every man that can take Robin Hood."

"No, Excellency," answered Robin. "I say without boasting that no man took Robin Hood yesterday, and none shall take him tomorrow."

Then he blew three loud blasts upon his own horn, drew out his own bow, and before the astonished Sheriff and his men could defend themselves, arrows were whistling in their midst.

Will Scarlet and Will Stutely had been watching ever since the Sheriff and Robin rode back toward Nottingham. Now in good time they came and the Sheriff's surprised force turned tail and ran, while Robin and his men sped swift arrows after them and laughed to see them go.

CHAPTER 10

How a Beggar Filled the Public Eye

"Good Robin accost him in his way,
To see what he might be;
If any beggar had money,
He thought some part had he."

ONE MORNING SOON AFTER his duel with Guy of Gisborne, Robin wandered alone down the road to see if the Sheriff had returned to search Sherwood. But all was still and peaceful. No one was in sight except a solitary beggar who was trudging along in Robin's direction. The beggar caught sight of Robin at the moment he emerged from the trees, but gave no sign of having seen him. He came forward merrily, whistling and beating time by punching holes in the dusty road with the stout staff in his hand.

The odd look of the fellow arrested Robin's attention and he decided to talk with him. The fellow was barelegged and barearmed, and over his shoulder he carried a heavy, bulging bag that was buckled by a leather strap. He had three hats upon his head, all tightly pulled together.

"Ha!" Robin thought to himself. "This is a lucky beggar for me! If any of them have money, this is the one, and he should share it with us poorer bodies."

So he flourished his own stick and planted himself in the traveler's path.

"Dear fellow!" said he, "where do you go so fast? Tarry, for I wish to speak with you!"

The beggar made as though he had not heard him and kept straight on his way.

"Tarry, I say!" said Robin again, "for there's a way to make folks obey!"

"Nay, 'tis not so," answered the beggar, speaking for the first time. "I obey no man in all England, not even the King himself. Let me pass on my way, for 'tis growing late, and I have still far to go before I can care for my stomach's good."

"Now, by my faith," said Robin, once more getting in front of the beggar, "I see that you do not lack for good food, while I go hungry. Therefore you must lend me some of your money till we meet again, so that I may eat at the nearest tavern."

"I have no money to lend," said the beggar crossly. "You are as young a man as I and as well able to earn a supper, so go your way and I'll go mine. If you wait to get anything out of me, you'll go hungry for the next twelve months."

"Not while I have a stout stick to whack your bones!" cried Robin. "Stand and deliver, I say, or I'll dust your shirt for you. And if that will not teach you manners, then we'll see what a broad arrow can do with a beggar's skin!"

The beggar smiled and answered boast with boast. "Come on with your staff, fellow! I care no more for it than for a pudding stick. And as for your pretty bow—that for it!"

And, with amazing quickness, he swung his staff around and knocked Robin's bow clean out of his hand, so that his fingers smarted with pain. Robin danced and tried to bring his own staff into action, but the beggar never gave him a chance. Biff! whack! came the staff, hitting him soundly and beating down his guard.

There were but two things to do: either stand there and take a sound drubbing or make a hasty retreat. Robin wisely chose the latter and scurried back into the wood, blowing his horn as he went.

"For shame!" jeered the beggar after him. "What is your haste? We had just begun. Stay and take your money or you will never be able to pay your reckoning at the tavern!"

But Robin never answered him a word. He fled up hill and down dale till he met three of his men, who were running up in answer to his summons.

"What is wrong?" they asked.

"'Tis a saucy beggar," said Robin, catching his breath. "He is back there on the high road, with the hardest stick I've met in a good many days. He would not give me a fair chance to deal with him."

The men—Much and two of the widow's sons—could scarcely conceal their laughter at the thought of Robin Hood running from a beggar. Nonetheless, they kept serious faces and asked their leader if he were hurt.

"Nay," he replied. "But I shall feel better if you

will fetch me that beggar and let me have a fair chance at him."

So the three yeomen hastened to the high road and followed after the beggar, who was going smoothly along his way as though he were at peace with all the world.

"The easiest way to settle this beggar," said Much, "is to surprise him. Let us cut through this neck of woods and come upon him before he is aware."

The others agreed to this and the three were soon close upon their prey.

"Now!" said Much. The other two sprang quickly upon the beggar's back and wrested his staff from his hand. At the same moment Much drew his dagger and flashed it in front of the beggar's face.

"Yield!" he cried. "A friend of ours awaits you in the wood to teach you how to fight properly."

"Give me a fair chance," said the beggar valiantly, "and I'll fight you all at once."

But they would not listen to him. Instead, they began to march him toward the forest. Seeing that it was useless to struggle, the beggar began to bargain.

"My good masters," said he, "why use this

violence? I will go with you quietly if you insist, but if you will set me free I'll make it worth your while. I've one hundred pounds in my bag here. Let me go my way and you shall have all that's in the bag."

The three outlaws took council together.

"What say you?" asked Much of the others. "Our master will be more glad to see this beggar's wallet than his sorry face."

The other two agreed and the little party came to a halt and let go of the beggar.

"Count out your gold, friend," said Much.

There was a brisk wind blowing and the beggar turned about to face it as soon as they unhanded him.

"It shall be done," said he. "One of you lend me your cloak and we will spread it upon the ground and put the wealth upon it."

The cloak was handed to him and he placed his bundle upon it as though it were very heavy indeed. Then he crouched down and fumbled with the leather fastenings. The outlaws also bent over and watched closely, in case he might hide some of the money on his person. Presently he got the bag unfastened and plunged his hands into it. From it he drew—not shining gold—

The·Four·Yeomen·haue·Merry· Sport·with·a·Stout·Miller:·

but handfuls of fine flour, which he threw into the eager faces of the men around him. The wind aided him in this and soon there arose a blinding cloud that filled the eyes, noses, and mouths of the three outlaws till they could scarcely see or breathe.

While they gasped and choked and sputtered and felt around wildly for the beggar, he finished the job by picking up the cloak by its corners and shaking it vigorously in their faces. Then he seized a stick that lay conveniently near and began to rain blows down upon their heads, shoulders, and sides, all the time dancing first on one leg, then on the other, and crying: "Villains! Rascals! Here are the hundred pounds I promised. How do you like them? You'll get all that's in the bag."

Whack! whack! whack! whack! went the stick, emphasizing each word. Howls of pain might have gone up from the sufferers, but they had too much flour in their throats for that. Their one thought was to flee, and they stumbled off blindly down the road, the beggar following them a little way to give them a few parting knocks.

"Farewell, my masters," he said finally, turning the other way. "And when next I come along the road I hope you will be able to tell gold from flour!"

With this he departed, an easy victor, and again went whistling on his way, while the three outlaws rubbed the flour out of their eyes and began to catch their breath again.

As soon as they could look around them clearly, they saw Robin Hood leaning against a tree trunk and watching them smilingly. He had recovered his own spirits on seeing their condition.

"God save you!" he said, "you must have been to the mill, from the look of your clothes."

When they answered not a word, he went on in a soft voice: "Did you see anything of that bold beggar I sent you for lately?"

"In truth, master," responded Much, the miller's son, "we heard more of him than we saw him. He filled us so full of flour that I shall sweat it for a week. I was born in a mill and had the smell of flour in my nostrils from my first birthday, and yet never before did I see such a quantity of the stuff in so small a space."

And he sneezed violently.

"How was that?" asked Robin.

"Why, when we laid hold of the beggar as you ordered, he offered to pay for his freedom out of the bag he carried upon his back."

"The same that I wanted," said Robin, as if to himself.

"So we agreed," went on Much, "and spread a cloak down and he opened his bag, and instantly a great cloud of flour filled the air so that we could neither see nor breathe, and in the midst of this cloud he vanished like a wizard."

"But not before he left certain black and blue spots to be remembered by, I see," Robin commented.

"He was in league with the devil," said one of the widow's sons, rubbing himself.

Then Robin laughed outright. "Four bold outlaws

put to shame by a sorry beggar!" cried he. "I can laugh at you, my men, for I am in the same boat with you. But it would never do to have this tale get about, even in the greenwood—how we could not hold our own with the odds in our favor. So let us have this little laugh all to ourselves and no one else need be the wiser!"

The others saw the point of this and none of the four ever told of the adventure. But the beggar must have boasted of it at the next tavern, or a little bird perched among the branches of a neighboring oak must have sung of it, for it got around, as such tales will, and was told about in a jesting ballad, which the four outlaws did not like to hear.

CHAPTER 11

How Robin Hood Came Before Queen Eleanor

"But Robin Hood, he himself had disguis'd,
  And Marian was strangely attir'd,
That they proved foes, and so fell to blows,
  Whose valor bold Robin admir'd.
 . . . . . .
"And when he came at London's court,
  He fell down on his knee.
'Thou art welcome, Lockesley,' said the Queen,
  'And all thy good yeomandree.'"

ONE DAY NOT LONG AFTER his meeting with the beggar, Robin decided to go hunting and, not knowing whom he might meet in his rambles, he stained his face and put on a sorry-looking cloak before he set out. As he walked, the peacefulness of the morning brought back to his memory the early days, so long ago, when he had roamed these same glades with Marian. How sweet they seemed to him now, and how far away! Marian, too—would he ever see her again? He had thought of her very often lately, wishing he could hear her musical laugh and see her eyes light up at his coming.

Perhaps the happiness of Allan-a-Dale and his lady caused Robin's heartstrings to vibrate more strongly. But Robin was certainly not thinking about hunting this bright morning as he walked along, his head drooping in a lovelorn way.

Presently a stag entered the glade in full view, grazing peacefully, and instantly Robin's bow was drawn. He had almost let go his arrow when the stag fell suddenly, struck by a shaft from the far side of the glade.

Then a handsome little **page** sprang from cover and ran towards the dying animal. This was plainly the archer, for he waved his bow above his head and also bore a sword at his side, though he looked a mere lad.

PAGE
A youth who is being trained for knighthood by serving a knight.

Robin approached from the other side.

"How dare you shoot the King's beasts?" he asked severely.

"I have as much right to shoot them as the King himself," answered the page. "How dare you question me?"

The voice stirred Robin strongly. It seemed to chime into his memories of the old days. He looked at the page sharply, and the page returned the glance, straight and unafraid.

"Who are you, lad?" Robin said more politely.

"No lad of yours, and my name's my own," answered the page with spirit.

"Softly, or we of the forest will have to teach you manners!" said Robin.

"Not if you stand for the forest!" cried the page, whipping out his sword. "Defend yourself!"

He swung his blade valiantly, and Robin saw nothing to do but to draw likewise. The page thereupon engaged him quite fiercely, and Robin found that the boy knew many tricks at fencing. Nonetheless, Robin contented himself with parrying and would not use his superior strength upon the lad. So the fight lasted for a quarter of an hour, at the end of which time the page was exhausted, and hot blood flushed his cheeks.

The outlaw saw his distress, and to end the fight allowed himself to be pricked slightly on the wrist.

"Are you satisfied, fellow?" asked the page, wincing a little at sight of the blood.

"Aye, honestly," replied Robin; "and now, perhaps, you will grant me the honor of knowing to whom I owe this scratch?"

"I am Richard Partington, page to Her Majesty Queen Eleanor," answered the lad with dignity, and again the sound of his voice troubled Robin sorely.

"Why do come you to Sherwood alone, Master Partington?"

The lad considered his answer while wiping his sword with a small lace handkerchief. The action brought a dim, confused memory to Robin. The lad finally looked him again in the eye.

"I seek Robin Hood, the outlaw, to whom I bring **amnesty** from the Queen. Can you tell me of him?" And while waiting for his answer he replaced the handkerchief in his shirt. As he did so, the gleam of a golden trophy caught the outlaw's eye.

AMNESTY
A pardon or forgiveness.

Robin started forward with a joyful cry.

"Ah! Now I know you! By the sight of that golden arrow won at the Sheriff's tourney, you are none other than Maid Marian!"

"You—are—?" gasped Marian, for it was she, "not Robin!"

"Robin himself!" said he gaily, and instantly, clad as he was in rags, and his face stained, he clasped the dainty page close to his breast, and she smiled happily.

"But Robin!" she exclaimed, "I did not recognize you and wounded you!"

"'Tis nothing," he replied laughingly, "so long as it brought me you."

But she made more fuss over the sore wrist than Robin had received for all his former wounds put together. She bound it with a little handkerchief and said: "Now it will get well!" and Robin never felt better in all his life.

But Marian, while happy also, was ill at ease. Robin, with a man's slow understanding, at last saw that it was because of her boy's attire. He smilingly handed her his tattered long cloak, which she blushingly put on and recovered her spirits directly.

Then they began to talk of each other's fortunes and the many things that had parted them, and so much did they find to tell that the sun sank well into the afternoon before they realized hours had passed.

"I am a sorry host!" exclaimed Robin, springing to his feet. "I have not invited you to my wild roof."

"And I am a sorry page," replied Marian. "I clean forgot that I really did bring you a message from Queen Eleanor!"

"Tell me on our way home. The first of my men we meet I will send back for your deer."

So she told him, as they walked back through the glade, how his fame had reached Queen Eleanor in London. And the Queen had said: "I wish that I could see this bold yeoman and his skill at the long bow." She promised him amnesty if he and four of his archers would come to London for the tournament the week following and shoot against **King Henry's** picked men, of whom the King was very vain. All this Marian told in detail, and added:

KING HENRY
King Henry II (1133-1189), the formal name of King Harry.

"When I heard Her Majesty say she desired to see you, I asked permission to go in search of you, saying I had known you once. The Queen was right glad, and she sent this gold ring to you from off her finger as a sign of her faith."

Then Robin took the ring, bowed his head, and kissed it loyally. "By this token I will go to London," said he, "and, before I part with the Queen's ring, may the hand that bears it be cut off at the wrist!"

By this time they had come to the grove before the cave, and Robin presented Maid Marian to the band, who treated her with the greatest respect. Will Scarlet was especially delighted to greet his old friend again, while Allan-a-Dale and his wife bustled about to make her welcome in their tiny thatched cottage.

That evening, after they had feasted royally upon the stag that Marian had slain, Allan sang sweet songs to their fair guest as she sat by Robin's side, the golden arrow gleaming in her dark hair. The others all joined in the chorus.

Then Robin asked Marian to repeat her message from the Queen. The yeomen gave three cheers for the Queen, and three more for her page, and drank toasts to them both, rising to their feet.

"You have heard," said Robin, standing up, "how

Her Majesty—God save her!—wishes four men to go with me. Therefore, I choose Little John and Will Stutely, my two lieutenants; Will Scarlet, my cousin, and Allan-a-Dale, my minstrel. Mistress Dale, also, can go with her husband and be company for the Queen's page. We will depart with early morning, decked out in our finest. So stir you, lads! And see that not only your tunics are fresh, but your swords bright and your bows and arrows fit. For we must be a credit to the Queen as well as to the greenwood. You, Much, with Stout Will, Lester, and John, shall have command of the band while we are away."

THE NEXT MORNING, as fine a summer's day as ever you want to see, Robin Hood had clothed his men in Lincoln green and himself in scarlet red, with black hats and white feathers for each head. Thus the party of seven set forth, accompanied to the edge of the wood by the whole band, who gave them a merry parting.

The journey to London was made without incident. They proceeded boldly along the King's high road and met no trouble. Besides, the Queen's warrant and ring would have answered for them, as, indeed, it did at the gates of London. So in due course they came to the palace itself and awaited an audience with the Queen.

Now, the King had gone that day to Finsbury Field, where the tourney was to be held, in order to see some of his picked men, whom he expected to win against all comers. So much had he boasted of these men that the Queen secretly resolved to win a wager from him. She had heard of the fame of Robin Hood and his yeomen, and Marian had been overjoyed to add a word in their favor and to set out in search of them.

Today the Queen sat in her private room, chatting pleasantly with her ladies, when in came Mistress Marian Fitzwalter, dressed again as a lady-in-waiting. She curtsied to the Queen and awaited permission to speak.

"Is this my lady Marian?" said the Queen, smiling, "or the page, Richard Partington?"

"Both, Your Majesty. Richard found the man you sought and Marian brought him to you."

"Where is he?" asked Queen Eleanor eagerly.

"Awaiting you—he and four of his men. Also a lady, of whose wedding I can tell you a pretty story at another time."

"Have them admitted."

So presently Robin Hood and his little party entered the room.

The Queen had expected the men to be uncouth in appearance because of their wild life in the forest, but she was delightfully disappointed. Indeed, she almost clapped her hands. To tell the truth, the yeomen made a brave sight, and in all the court no more gallant men could be found. Marian felt her cheeks glow with pride at the looks of admiration from the other ladies-in-waiting.

Robin did not forget the gentle manners his mother taught him, and he wore his fine red velvet tunic and breeches with the grace of a courtier. We have seen before what a gentleman Will Scarlet could be; and Allan-a-Dale, the minstrel, was scarcely less handsome to look upon, while the giant Little John and broad-shouldered Will Stutely made up in stature what little they lacked in outward polish. Mistress Dale looked even more charming than on the day when she went to Plympton Church to marry one man and found another.

Robin advanced, knelt down before her, and said:

"Here I am, Robin Hood, I and my chosen men! At Your Majesty's bidding I've come, bearing the ring of amnesty, which I will protect—as I would protect Your Majesty's honor—with my life!"

"Thou art welcome, Lockesley," said the Queen, smiling graciously. "Thou art come in good time."

Then Robin presented each of his men in turn, and each fell on his knee and was greeted with kind words. The Queen kissed Mistress Dale on the cheek and asked her to remain in the palace with her ladies while she was in the city. Fine wines were brought, and cake, and rich food, for their refreshment. And as they ate and drank, the Queen told them about the tournament to be held at Finsbury Field, and of how she desired them to wear her colors and shoot for her. Meantime, she said, they were to stay quiet and out of sight.

To all of this Robin and his men pledged themselves. Then, at the Queen's request, they told her and her ladies some of their adventures. The listeners were greatly entertained and laughed often. Then Marian, who had heard of the wedding at Plympton Church, told the story so humorously that tears stood in the Queen's eyes.

"My lord Bishop of Hereford!" she said. "It was, indeed, a comical business for him! I shall keep that to

ALLAN·A·DALE·SINGETH·BE=
FORE·OVR·GOOD·QVEEN·EL=
EANOR·   ·MDCCCXXCIII·

twit him, I promise you! So this is our minstrel?" she added, turning to Allan-a-Dale. "I think I have already heard of him. Will he not play his harp for us today?"

Allan bowed low, took a harp that was brought to him, and strummed the strings and sang sweetly the songs of the North Country. And the Queen and all her ladies listened in silence till all the songs were ended.

CHAPTER 12

How the Outlaws Shot in King Harry's Tournament

"The King is into Finsbury Field
Marching in battle 'ray;
And after follows bold Robin Hood,
And all his yeomen gay."

THE MORNING OF the great archery contest brought a fever of impatience to every citizen of London. All the surrounding country folk were awake early and began to make their way to Finsbury Field, a broad stretch of practice ground near Moorfields. Around three sides of the Field tier upon tier of seats were erected for the spectators, with the royal boxes and booths for the nobility and gentry in the center. Down along one end were pitched gaily-colored tents for the different bands of King's archers. There were ten of these bands, each containing a score of men, headed by a captain. So today there were ten pavilions, each flying the Royal Arms and varicolored pennants which fluttered in the fresh morning breeze.

Each captain's flag was of peculiar color and **device**. First came the royal purple streamer of Tepus, bow bearer to the King and esteemed as the finest archer in all England. Then came the yellow of Clifton of Buckinghamshire; and the blue of Gilbert of the White Hand, who was famous in Nottinghamshire; and the green of Elwyn, the Welshman; and the white of Robert of Cloudesdale; and, after them, five other captains of bands, each a man of proved skill. As the Queen had said, the King was extremely proud of his archers and held this tournament to show their skill and, perhaps, to recruit their forces.

DEVICE
The design or emblem that identified a person or family; a coat-of-arms

The tiers of seats filled early, and the merry chatter of the people hummed like bees in a hive. In and out among the seats went hawkers selling small pennants to correspond with the rival tents. Other vendors of pies and small cakes and cider also did a pretty business. So eager had some of the people been to get good seats, that they had rushed away from home without their breakfast.

Suddenly the gates at the far end opened wide, and a rider in scarlet and gold, mounted upon a white horse, rode in blowing lustily upon a trumpet, and behind him came six flagbearers riding abreast. The people rose with a mighty cheer as King Harry entered the arena. He rode a fine white charger and was clad in a rich dark suit of velvet with satin and gold facings. His hat had a long curling ostrich plume of pure white, and he lifted it graciously to answer to the shouts of the people. By his side rode Queen Eleanor, while immediately behind them came Prince Richard and Prince John, each in knightly coats of mail and helmets. Lords and ladies of the realm followed and, finally, the ten companies of archers, whose progress round the field was greeted with hardly less applause than that given the King himself.

The King and Queen dismounted from their steeds, climbed the steps of the royal box, and seated themselves upon two thrones, decked with purple and gold trappings, on a platform sheltered by striped canvas.

The herald rose, and the clear note of his trumpet hushed the crowd to silence. The archers ranged themselves in two long rows on each side of the **lists**, while their captains, as a special mark of favor, stood near the royal box.

"Come, Tepus," said the King. "Come, measure me out this line, how long our mark must be."

"What is the reward?" then asked the Queen.

"For first prize we have offered a purse containing forty gold pounds," answered the King. "For second, a purse containing forty silver pennies, and for third, a silver bugle inlaid with gold. Moreover, if the King's companies keep these prizes, the winning companies shall have first, two casks of Rhine wine; second, two casks of English beer; and, third, five fat harts."

LISTS
In tournaments, a fenced area where knights on horseback charged each other and each tried to knock his opponent from his horse with a lance.

HARTS
Male deer.

"Get a line of good length, Tepus," said the King, "and set up the targets at two hundred paces."

Tepus bowed low and set up ten targets, each bearing the pennant of a different company, while the herald proclaimed the rules and prizes. The entries were open to all comers. Each man, also, of the King's archers would shoot three arrows at the target bearing the colors of his band, until the best bowman in each band was chosen. These ten chosen archers would then enter a contest for an open target—three shots apiece—and at that time any other bowman could try his skill. The result at the open targets would decide the tournament.

Then the archers waved their bows aloft and faced their respective targets.

The shooting now began at all the targets at once, and the crowd had so much to watch that they forgot to shout. Besides, silence was commanded during the shooting. The full score of men shot three times at

each target, and then three times again to decide a tie—
for, more than once, the arrow shot by one man would be
split wide open by the archer who shot next. Every man's
arrow bore his number to ease the counting, and they
were so close at the end of a round that the target looked
like a big bristle hairbrush.

At last the company targets were decided and
Tepus, as expected, led the score, having made six exact
centers in a row. Gilbert of the White Hand followed
with five and Clifton with four. Two other captains had
touched their center four times. In the other companies
it so happened that the captains had been outshot by
some of the men under them.

The winners then saluted the King and Queen
and withdrew to rest and change their bowstrings for the
keenest contest of all. A new target—the open one— was
set up at two hundred and fifty paces. On the orders of
the King, the herald announced that the open target was
to be shot at to decide the title of the best archer in all
England, and any man there might try for it. But the pre-
vious shooting had been so keen that many yeomen who
had come to enter the contest now would not do so, and
only a dozen men stepped forward to give their names.

"These must be hardy men to pit themselves against my archers!" said the King.

"Do you think your ten fellows are the best bowmen in England?" asked the Queen.

"Aye, and in all the world besides," answered the King, "and I will stake five hundred pounds on it."

"I am inclined to take your wager," said the Queen, "and will do so if you grant me a favor."

"What is it?" asked the King.

"If I find five archers who can outshoot your ten, will you grant my men full amnesty?"

"Absolutely!" said the King in good humor. "I tell you now your wager is in jeopardy, for there never were better bowmen than Tepus and Clifton and Gilbert!"

"Hmm!" said the Queen, puckering her brow as though lost in thought. "I must see if anyone present can aid me in my wager. Boy, call Sir Richard of the Lea and the Bishop of Hereford here!"

They came forward.

"Sir Richard," she said, "would you advise me to agree to a wager with the King that I can produce other archers as good as Tepus and Gilbert and Clifton?"

"Nay, Your Majesty," he said, bending his knee.

"None present can match them. Though," he added, dropping his voice, "I have heard of some who hide in Sherwood Forest who could show them strange targets."

The Queen smiled, and dismissed him.

"My lord Bishop of Hereford," said she. "Would you advance a sum to support my wager against the King?"

"Nay, Your Majesty," said the fat Bishop. "If you pardon me, I'd not put down a penny on such a bet, for the King's archers have no peers."

"But suppose I found men whom you knew to be masters at archery," she insisted. "Would you not back them? I have heard that there are such men round Nottingham and Plympton!"

The Bishop glanced nervously around, as if half expecting to see Robin Hood's men standing near, then turned to find the Queen looking at him with amusement lurking in her eyes.

The story of Allan-a-Dale's wedding must have preceded me! he thought, regretfully. Aloud he said, resolved to face it out: "Your Majesty, such tales are exaggerated. If you pardon me, I will add to the King's wager that his men are invincible."

"As you please," replied the Queen. "How much?"

"Here is my purse," said the Bishop uneasily. "It contains nearly a hundred pounds."

"I'll take it at even money," she said, dismissing him. "And, Your Majesty," said the Queen, turning to the King, "I accept your wager of five hundred pounds."

"Very good," said the King, laughing as though it were great fun. "But why do you take such interest in the sport of a sudden?"

"As I have said. I have found five men whom I will pit against any you may produce."

"Then we will try their skill," said the King. "First, let us decide this open target and then match the five best at it against your mysterious champions."

"Agreed," said the Queen. She signaled to Maid Marian to step forward from a nearby booth where she sat with other ladies-in-waiting and whispered something in her ear. Marian curtsied and withdrew.

The ten winning archers from the King's bands came forward again, and with them stood twelve men from the open lists. Again the crowd was stilled, and every eye hung upon the speeding shafts. Slowly but skillfully each man shot, and as his shaft struck in the inner ring a deep breath broke from the crowd like the sound of the wind upon the seashore. Gilbert of the White Hand led the shooting, and it was only by the space of a hairsbreadth on the line that Tepus tied his score. Elwyn, the Welshman, took third place. One of the private archers, named Geoffrey, came in fourth; while Clifton must content himself with fifth. The men from the open lists shot fairly true, but nervousness brought their undoing.

The herald then came forward again and, instead of announcing the prizewinners, proclaimed that there was to be another contest. Two men had tied for first place, the King had declared, and the three others were entitled to honors. Now all these five were to shoot again and they were to be matched against five others of the Queen's choosing—men who had not yet shot that day.

A thrill of astonishment and excitement swept the arena. "Who were these men of the Queen's?" was on every lip. The hubbub of voices grew intense, and in the midst of it all the gate at the far end of the field opened and five men entered, escorting a lady on horseback across the arena to the royal box. The lady was instantly recognised as Mistress Marian, but no one seemed to know the faces of her escort. Four were clad in Lincoln green, while the fifth, who seemed to be the leader, was dressed in a suit of scarlet red. Each man wore a closefitting cap of black, with a curling white feather. For weapons, they carried simply a bow, a sheaf of new arrows, and a short hunting knife.

When the little party came before the platform on which the King and Queen sat, the yeomen raised their caps humbly, while Maid Marian dismounted.

"Your Gracious Majesty," she said, addressing the Queen. "These are the men for whom you sent me and who are now come to wear your colors and serve you in the tournament."

The Queen leaned forward and handed them each a scarf of green and gold.

"Lockesley," she said in a clear voice, "I thank thee and thy men for this service. I have laid a wager with the King that you can outshoot the five best of all his bowmen."

The five men pressed the scarves to their lips to show their loyalty.

The King turned to the Queen inquiringly.

"Who are these men?" he asked.

Up came the Bishop of Hereford, growing red.

"Your pardon, my lord!" he cried. "But I must denounce these fellows as outlaws. That man in scarlet is none other than Robin Hood himself. The others are Little John and Will Stutely and Will Scarlet and Allan-a-Dale—all famous in the North Country for their deeds of violence."

"As my lord Bishop personally knows!" added the Queen.

The King's brows grew dark. The name Robin Hood was well known to every man there.

"Is this true?" he demanded sternly.

"Aye, my lord," responded the Queen calmly. "But I have your royal promise of amnesty."

"That I will keep," said the King, holding his anger in check by a mighty effort. "But I grant only forty days of amnesty. When this time has passed, let these outlaws look to their safety!"

Then turning to his five victorious archers, who had drawn near, he added: "You have heard, my men, how I have a wager with the Queen upon your skill. Now, here are men of her choosing. Look well to it,

Gilbert and Tepus and Geoffrey and Elwyn and Clifton! If you outshoot these knaves I will fill your caps with silver pennies, aye, and knight the man who stands first. But if you lose I must give the prizes to Robin Hood and his men, according to my royal word."

"Robin Hood and his men!" The saying flew round the arena with the speed of wildfire, and every neck craned forward to see the famous fellows who dared to face the King's anger because of the Queen.

Another target was now set up, at the same distance as the last, and it was decided that the ten archers should shoot three arrows in turn. Gilbert and Robin tossed up a penny for the lead, and it fell to the King's men, so Clifton was to shoot first. He planted his feet firmly and licked his fingers before plucking the string, for he was determined to better the score he had earlier. And in truth he did so. His shaft sped true and landed on the black bull's-eye, though not in the exact center. Again he shot, and again he hit the black, on the opposite rim. The third shaft swerved downward and hit in the second ring. Nonetheless, a general cry went up. This was the best shooting Clifton had done that day.

Will Scarlet was chosen to follow him; he now

took his place and carefully chose three arrows.

"Careful, cousin!" said Robin in a low tone. "He has left wide space at the center for all of your darts."

But Robin gave Will the wrong caution. Too much care spoiled his aim. His first arrow flew wide and lodged in the second ring, even farther away than Clifton's worst shot.

"I beg your pardon, cousin!" said Robin. "Let go of your string before it sticks to your fingers!"

And Will loosed his next two shafts as freely as if they flew along a Sherwood glade. Each struck the bull's-eye, and one even nearer the center than his rival's mark, but the total score was still in favor of Clifton. At this Will Scarlet bit his lip but said no word, while the crowd shouted and waved yellow flags for joy that the King's man had overcome the outlaw. They knew, also, that this demonstration would please the King.

The target was now cleared for the next two contestants—Geoffrey and Allan-a-Dale. Geoffrey had shot many good shafts that day, but each of his three shots, though well placed around the rim of the bull's-eye, yet allowed space for Allan to graze within. Allan's shooting, moreover, was so prettily done that he was heartily applauded—the ladies leading in the clapping.

Now, there had long been a friendly rivalry in Robin Hood's band as to who was the best shot after Robin himself. Second place lay between Little John and Stutely, and neither wished to yield to the other, so today they looked narrowly at their leader to see who should shoot third. Robin read their faces at a glance and, laughing merrily, broke off two straws and held them out.

"The long straw goes next!" he decided—Stutely drew it.

Elwyn, the Welshman, preceded him, and his score was no better than Geoffrey's. But Stutely failed to profit by it. His failing at archery had always been haste and carelessness. Today these were increased by a certain moodiness that Little John had outranked him. So his first two shafts flew swiftly, one after the other, to places outside the Welshman's mark.

"Man! man!" cried Robin. "You forget the honor of the Queen and of Sherwood!"

"I ask your pardon, master!" said Will humbly, and as he spoke he let fly his last shaft. It whistled down the course and struck in the exact center—the best shot yet made.

Some shouted for Stutely and some shouted for Elwyn, but Elwyn's total mark was declared the better. Then the King turned to the Queen.

"What do you say now?" said he in some triumph. "Two out of the three first rounds have gone to my men. Your outlaws will have to shoot better than that in order to save your wager!"

The Queen smiled gently.

"Yes, my lord," she said, "but the two who are left are able to do the shooting. I still have Little John and Robin Hood."

"And you forget, my lady, that I still have Tepus and Gilbert."

So each awaited the next rounds in silent eagerness.

Tepus was chosen to go next, and he fell into the same error as Will Scarlet. He held the string a moment too long, and both his first and second arrows landed off center. One of them, however, came within the black rim, and he followed it up by placing his third in the full center, just as Stutely had done with his last. These two centers were the best shots that had been made that day, and loud applause greeted this second one. But the shouting was as nothing to the uproar that followed Little John's shooting. That good-natured giant seemed determined to outdo Tepus by a tiny margin in each separate shot, for the first and the second shafts grazed his rival's on the inner side, while for the third Little John did the old trick of the forest: he shot his own arrow in a graceful curve, which descended from above upon Tepus's final center shaft with a glancing blow that drove the other out and left the outlaw's in its place.

The King could scarcely believe his eyes. "By all that is sacred!" said he, "that fellow deserves either a dukedom or a hanging! He must be in league with Satan himself! I never saw such shooting before."

"The score is tied, my lord," said the Queen; "we have still to see Gilbert and Robin Hood."

Gilbert now took his stand and slowly shot his arrows, one after another, into the bull's-eye. It was the best shooting he had done yet; but there was still the smallest of spaces left—if you looked closely—at the very center.

"Well done, Gilbert!" said Robin Hood. "Now, if you had placed one of your shafts there"—loosing one of his own—"and another there"—out sped the second—"and another there"—the third was launched—"perhaps the King would have declared you the best bowman in all England!"

But the last part of his speech was drowned in a wild tumult of applause. His first two shafts had packed themselves into the small space left at the bull's-eye, while his third had split between them, taking half of each, and making all three appear from a distance as one immense arrow.

Up rose the King in amazement and anger.

"Gilbert is not yet beaten!" he cried. "Did he not shoot within the mark three times? And that is allowed a tie in all the rules of archery."

Robin bowed low.

"As it please Your Majesty!" said he. "But may I be allowed to place the mark for the second shooting?"

The King waved his hand sullenly. Then Robin prepared another old trick of the greenwood and got a light, peeled willow branch, which he set in the ground as a target.

"There, friend Gilbert," called he gaily. "Perhaps you can hit that!"

"I can scarcely see it from here," said Gilbert,

"much less hit it. But, for the King's honor, I will try."

But this final shot proved his undoing, and his shaft flew harmlessly by the thin white streak. Then Robin came to his stand again, picked his arrow with great care, and tried his string. The crowd was silent as he drew the good yew bow back to his ear, glanced along the shaft, and let the feathered missile fly. Straight it sped, singing a note of triumph as it went. The willow wand was split in two, as though it had been sliced by a hunter's knife.

"Verily, I think your bow is aided by witchcraft," cried Gilbert. "I did not believe such shooting possible."

"You should come see our merry lads in the greenwood," answered Robin lightly. "Willow wands do not grow on the cobblestones of London."

Meanwhile the King, in great anger, had risen to depart, first signing to the judges to distribute the prizes. He never said a word, good or ill, to the Queen, but mounted his horse and, followed by his sons and knights, rode off the field. The archers dropped upon one knee as he passed, but he gave them a short, sinister look and was gone.

Then the Queen beckoned the outlaws to

approach, and they knelt at her feet.

"Right well have you served me," she said, "and sorry am I that the King's anger is aroused by it. But fear not, his word holds true. As to these prizes you have won, I add others of my own—the wagers I have won from His Majesty the King and from the lord Bishop of Hereford. Buy with some of this money the best swords you can find in London for all your band, call them the swords of the Queen, and swear with them to protect all the poor and helpless, and all the women who come your way."

"We swear," said the five yeomen solemnly.

Then the Queen gave each of them her hand to kiss, and arose, and departed with all her ladies. And after they were gone the King's archers came crowding around Robin and his men, eager to get a glimpse of the fellows about whom they had heard so much. And behind them came a great crowd of the spectators, pushing and jostling to come nearer.

Next the judges came up and announced to each man his prize, according to the King's command. Robin was given the purse containing forty golden pounds, to Little John went the forty silver pennies, and to Allan-a-

Dale the fine inlaid bugle, much to his delight, but when the Rhine wine and English beer and harts were spoken of, Robin said:

"Nay, what need we of wine or beer so far from the greenwood? And it would be like **carrying coals to Newcastle** to drive those harts to Sherwood! Now, Gilbert and Tepus and their men have shot well—therefore the meat and drink must go to them, if they will accept it from us."

"Right gladly," replied Gilbert, grasping his hand. "You are good men all, and we will toast you every one, in memory of the greatest day at archery that England has ever seen!"

CARRYING COALS TO NEWCASTLE
To do something unnecessary. Newcastle is an English port noted for shipping coal.

CHAPTER 13

How Robin Hood Was Sought by a Tinker

"And while the tinker fell asleep,
Robin made haste away,
And left the tinker in the lurch,
For the great shot to pay."

K ING HARRY KEPT HIS WORD. Robin Hood and his men were allowed to depart from London—the parting bringing keen sorrow to Marian—and for forty days no hand was raised against them. But at the end of that time the King sent word to the Sheriff at Nottingham that he must capture the outlaws without further delay if he valued his office.

Indeed, the exploits of Robin and his band, ending with the great tourney at Finsbury Field, had made a

mighty stir through all England, and many laughed at
the Nottingham sheriff for his failures.

The Sheriff planned three new expeditions into
the greenwood and was even brave enough to lead them,
since he had three hundred men at his beck and call each
time. But he never saw the shadow of an outlaw, for
Robin's men lay close, and the Sheriff's men could not
find their chief hiding-place.

NOW THE SHERIFF'S DAUGHTER had hated Robin
Hood bitterly ever since the day he refused to bestow the
golden arrow upon her and so shamed her before all the
people. His tricks, also, upon her father did not lessen
her hatred, and so she sought ways for the Sheriff to
catch the outlaw.

"There is no need to go against this man with
force of arms," she said to her father. "We must meet his
tricks with tricks of our own."

"I wish that we could," groaned the Sheriff. "The
fellow is a nightmare to me."

"Let me plan awhile," she replied. "Perhaps I can
cook up some scheme."

"Agreed," said the Sheriff, "and if anything

comes of your planning I will even give you a hundred silver pennies for a new gown and a double reward to the man who catches the outlaw."

Now on that same day, while the Sheriff's daughter was racking her brains for a scheme, a **tinker** named Middle, a great gossip and braggart, came to the Mansion House. And as he pounded away upon some pots and pans in the kitchen, he talked loudly about what he would do if he once came within reach of Robin Hood.

TINKER Someone who repaired metal household utensils.

It might be that this fool could succeed because of his very stupidity, thought the Sheriff's daughter, overhearing his bragging.

And she called him to her and looked him over— a big, brawny fellow with an honest look about the eye.

"I am minded to try your skill at outlaw catching," she said, "and will add generously to the stated reward if you succeed. Do you wish to make good your boasts?"

The tinker grinned broadly.

"Yes, your ladyship," he said.

"Then here is a warrant made out this morning by the Sheriff himself. See that you keep it safely and use it to good advantage."

And she dismissed him.

Middle departed mightily pleased with himself and proud of his commission. He swung his crabtree staff recklessly in his glee and vowed he'd crack the ribs of Robin Hood with it even if he was surrounded by every outlaw in Sherwood Forest.

Spurred on by thoughts of his bravery, he left the town and proceeded towards Barnesdale. The day was hot and dusty and at noon he paused at an inn to refresh himself. He began by eating and drinking and then dozing.

The innkeeper of the "Blue Boar" stood by, discussing Robin with a cattle driver.

"Folks say that the Sheriff has sent to Lincoln for more soldiers and horses and that when he has these behind him he'll soon rid the forest of these fellows."

"Of whom are you speaking?" asked the tinker, sitting up.

"Of Robin Hood and his men," said the innkeeper. "But go to sleep again—you will never get the reward!"

"And why not?" asked the tinker, rising with great show of dignity.

"Where our Sheriff has failed, and Guy of Gisborne and many more besides, no mere tinker will succeed."

The tinker laid a heavy hand upon the innkeeper's fat shoulder and tried to look impressive.

"There is your reckoning, innkeeper, upon the table. I must go upon my way, because I have more important business than to stand here gossiping with you. But do not be surprised if the next time you see me, I have with me Robin Hood himself!"

And he strode out the door and walked up the hot road towards Barnesdale.

He had not gone a quarter of a mile when he met a young man with curling brown hair and merry eyes. The young man carried his light cloak over his arm because of the heat, and was unarmed save for a light sword at his side. He eyed the perspiring tinker in a friendly way and, seeing he was a stout fellow, spoke to him.

"Good day to you!" said he.

"Good day to you!" said the tinker, "and a morrow less hot."

"Aye," laughed the other. "Where do you come from? And know you the news?"

"What is the news?" said the gossipy tinker, pricking up his ears. "I am a tinker by trade, Middle by name, and come from over near Banbury."

"Why, as for the news," laughed the stranger, "I hear that two tinkers were set in the stocks for drinking too much ale and beer."

"All I have to tell," said the other, "is that I am especially commissioned"—he felt mightily proud of these words—"especially commissioned to seek the outlaw they call Robin Hood."

"So?" said the other, arching his brows. "How 'especially commissioned'?"

"I have a warrant from the Sheriff, sealed with the King's own seal, to take him where I can, and if you can tell me where he is, I will make a man of you."

"Let me see the warrant," said the young man, "to satisfy myself if it be right, and I will do the best I can to bring him to you."

"That I will not," replied the tinker. "I trust none with it. And if you'll not help me, then I must catch him by myself."

And he made his crabtree staff whistle circles in the air.

Robin·and·the·Tinker:
at·the·
BLUE·BOAR·INN:

The other smiled, and said: "The middle of the road on a hot July day is not a good place to talk things over. Now, if you're the man for me and I'm the man for you, let's go back to the inn, just beyond the bend of road, and quench our thirst and cool our heads for thinking."

"That will I!" said the tinker. "For though I've just come from there, my thirst rises mightily at the sound of your voice."

So back he turned with the stranger and proceeded to the Blue Boar Inn.

The landlord arched his eyebrows silently when he saw the two come in, but served them willingly.

The tinker asked for wine and Robin for ale. Wine was not the most cooling drink in the cellars nor the clearest-headed. Nonetheless, the tinker asked for it, since it was expensive and the other man had invited him to drink. They lingered long over their cups, Master Middle emptying one after another, while the stranger talked at great length on the best plans for capturing Robin Hood.

In the end the tinker fell sound asleep while in the act of trying to get a tankard to his lips. Then the stranger deftly opened the snoring man's pouch, took out the warrant, read it, and put it in his own wallet. Calling the host to him, he winked at him with a half smile and told him that the tinker would pay the whole bill when he awoke. Thus Middle was left in the lurch.

Still, the stranger seemed in no great hurry. He had the whim to stay awhile and see what the tinker might do when he awoke. So he hid outside behind a window shutter and waited.

Presently the tinker awoke with a mighty yawn and reached at once for another drink.

"What were you saying, friend, about the best plan—yaaaah!—for catching this fellow? Hello! Where's he gone?"

He could see no one with him at the table and looked round.

"Host! host!" he shouted, "where is that fellow who was to pay my reckoning?"

"I know not," answered the landlord sharply. "Perhaps he left the money in your purse."

"No, he didn't!" roared Middle, looking there. "Help! Help! I've been robbed! Look you, host, you are liable to arrest for high treason! I am here upon the

King's business, as I told you earlier in the day. And yet while I did rest under your roof, thinking you were an honest man—hic!—and one loving the King, my pouch has been opened and matters of State taken from it."

"Cease your bellowing!" said the landlord. "What did you lose?"

"Oh, many weighty matters, I do assure you. I had with me: item, a warrant granted under the hand of my lord High Sheriff of Nottingham and sealed with the King's own seal for the capture—hic!—and arrest of a notorious rascal, one Robin Hood of Sherwood. Item, one crust of bread. Item, one lump—hic!—of **solder**. Item, three pieces of twine. Item, six single keys—hic! Item, twelve silver pennies, which I earned this week—hic!—in fair labor. Item—"

SOLDER
A mixture of tin and lead that is melted to bond two pieces of metal together.

"Enough of your 'items'!" said the host. "I marvel greatly to hear you speak in such fashion of your friend Robin Hood. For was he not with you just now, and did he not drink with you in good fellowship?"

"What? Robin Hood?" gasped Middle, with staring eyes. "Why did you not tell me?"

"Faith, I saw no need of telling you! Did you not tell me the first time you were here today that I need not be surprised if you came back with none other than Robin Hood himself?"

"I see it all now," moaned the tinker. "He got me to drinking and then took my warrant and my pennies and my crust."

"Yes, yes," interrupted the host. "I know all about that. Now you must pay me the bill for both of you."

"But I have no money. Let me go after that sly bag of bones and I'll soon get it out of him."

"If I waited for you to collect from Robin Hood," replied the other, "I would soon close up shop."

"What is the account?" asked Middle, discouraged.

"Ten shillings."

"Then take my bag and my good hammer too, and if I find that knave I will soon come back after them."

"Give me your leather coat as well," said the host. "The hammer and tools are nothing to me."

"Mercy!" cried Middle, losing what was left of his temper. "It seems that I escaped one thief only to fall into the hands of another. If you will walk with me out into the middle of the road I'll give you such a crack that will drive some honesty into your thick skull."

"You are wasting your breath and my time," retorted the landlord. "Give me your things and get gone after your man speedily."

Middle thought this was good advice, so he left the Blue Boar in a black mood.

Before he had gone half a mile he saw Robin Hood walking calmly a little ahead of him.

"Ho, there, you villain!" roared the tinker. "Stay your steps! I am desperately in need of you!"

Robin turned about with a surprised face.

"What knave is this," he asked gently, "who comes shouting after me?"

"No knave at all!" panted the other, rushing up, "but an honest man who would have that warrant and the money for drink!"

"Why, as I live, it is our honest tinker who was seeking Robin Hood! Did you find him?"

"Indeed, that did I! And I'm now going to pay him my respects!"

And he plunged at him, making a sweeping

stroke with his crabtree cudgel.

Robin tried to draw his sword, but could not do it for a moment while he dodged the other's furious blows. Before he did get it in hand, the tinker had reached him three times with resounding thwacks. Then the tables were turned as Robin dashed at the tinker with his shining blade and made him retreat.

The greenwood rang with the noise of the fray. It was steel against wood, and they made a terrible clattering when they came together. Robin thought at first that he could hack the cudgel to pieces, for his blade was one of finely tempered steel—which the Queen had given him. But the crabtree staff had been fired and hardened and seasoned by the tinker's arts until it was like a bar of iron—no pleasant neighbor for one's ribs.

Robin presently found this out to his sorrow. The long reach and long stick got to him when it was impossible for him to touch his antagonist, so his sides began to ache sorely.

"Hold your hand, tinker," he said at length. "I beg a favor of you."

"Before I do it," said the tinker, "I'll hang you on this tree."

But as he spoke, Robin found the moment's grace for which he longed and immediately grasped his horn and blew the three well-known blasts.

"Up to your old tricks, are you?" roared the tinker, starting up afresh. "Well, I'll have time to finish my job if I hurry."

But Robin was quite able to hold his own and they had not exchanged many strokes when up came Little John and Will Scarlet and a score of yeomen at their heels. Middle was seized instantly, while Robin sat down to breathe.

"What is the matter?" said Little John, "that ye should sit so on the highway side?"

"That rascally tinker yonder has paid his bill well upon my hide," answered Robin.

"That tinker, then," said Little John, "must be itching for more work. Can he do as much for me?"

"Or me," said Will Scarlet, who, like Little John, was always willing to swing a cudgel.

"Nay," laughed Robin. "Perhaps I could have done better if he had given me time to pull a young tree up; but I hated to spoil the Queen's blade upon his tough stick. Besides, he had a good quarrel with me. He had a warrant for my arrest, which I stole from him."

"Also: Item, twelve silver pennies," interposed the tinker, insistently. "Item, one crust of bread, my supper. Item, one lump of solder. Item, three pieces of twine. Item, six single keys. Item—"

"Yes, I know," said merry Robin. "I stood outside the Blue Boar's window and heard you count over your losses. Here they are again and the twelve silver pennies are turned by magic into gold. Here also, if you will, is my hand."

"I take it gladly, with the pennies!" cried Middle. "And so shall I have my leather coat and tools presently from that sly host. Now, I swear that I never yet met a man I liked as well as you! If you and your men here will take me, I swear I'll serve you honestly. Do you want a tinker? Verily you must! Who else can mend and grind your swords and fight, too, when need be? And mend your pots and mend your pans!"

"What do say you, fellows?" asked Robin. "Would not this tinker be a good recruit?"

"That he would," answered Will Scarlet, clapping the new man on the back. "He will keep Friar Tuck and Much, the miller's son, from having the blues."

So amid great merriment and good fellowship the outlaws shook Middle by the hand; he took the oath of loyalty and never thought more of the Sheriff's daughter.

CHAPTER 14

How Robin Hood Met Sir Richard of the Lea

"Then answered him the gentle knight
With words both fair and free:
'God save thee, my good Robin,
And all thy company!'"

MONTHS PASSED AS WINTER dragged wearily through Sherwood Forest. Robin Hood and his merry men found what cheer they could in the big crackling fires before their woodland cave. Friar Tuck had built a little hermitage not far away, where he lived comfortably with his numerous dogs.

At last the blessed spring came—and went. Another summer passed, and still neither King nor Sheriff nor Bishop could catch the outlaws, who, meanwhile, prospered mightily. The band had been increased from time to time by picked men such as Arthur-a-Bland until it now numbered a full seven companies, each with its lieutenant serving under Robin Hood. And still they relieved the rich of their purses, and aided the poor, and feasted upon King's deer, until the Sheriff of Nottingham was nearly insane.

Indeed, the Sheriff would probably have lost his office had it not been for the fact of the King's death. Henry passed away, as all kings will, like ordinary men, and Richard the Lion Hearted was proclaimed as his successor.

Then Robin and his men, after earnest debate, resolved to throw themselves upon the mercy of the new King, swear allegiance, and ask to be accepted as Royal Foresters. So Will Scarlet and Will Stutely and Little John were sent to London with this message, which they were first to give privately to Maid Marian. But they soon returned with bad tidings. The new King was still gone on a Crusade to the Holy Land, and Prince John, his brother, was impossible to deal with—being crafty, cruel, and treacherous. He was laying his hands upon all the property that could easily be seized, including the estates of the Earl of Huntingdon, Robin's old enemy and Marian's father, who had lately died.

Marian herself was in trouble. Her estates had been taken away. She had lost the protection of the former Queen, and the evil Prince John tormented her with his attentions. He thought that since Marian was defenseless, he could carry her away to one of his castles and no one could prevent him.

No word of this peril reached Robin's ears, although his men brought him news of the seizure of the Huntingdon lands. Nonetheless, he was greatly alarmed for the safety of Maid Marian, and his heart cried out for her strongly. She had been continually in his thoughts ever since the tournament at London.

One morning in early autumn, when the leaves were turning gold at the edges and the whole wide woodland was scented with the ripe fragrance of fruit, Robin was walking along the edge of a small glade busy with his thoughts. The peace of the woods was upon him, despite his broodings over Marian, and he paid little notice to a group of does quietly feeding at the far edge of the glade.

But suddenly a stag, wild and furious, dashed from among the trees, scattering the does. The vicious beast eyed Robin's green-and-gold tunic and, lowering its head, charged at him. So sudden was its attack that Robin had no time to bend his bow. He sprang behind a tree while he fixed an arrow upon the string.

A moment later the stag crashed blindly into the tree trunk with a shock that sent the beast reeling backward, while leaves from the shivering tree fell in a small shower over Robin's head.

He saw the stag turn about and fix its glance rigidly on the bushes to the left side of the glade. These were parted by a delicate hand and through the opening appeared the slight figure of a page. It was Maid Marian, who had come back to Sherwood!

She stepped forward, unaware of Robin's horrified gaze or the evil fury of the stag.

She was directly in line with the animal, so Robin dared not launch an arrow. Her own bow was slung across her shoulder, and her small sword would be useless against the beast's charge.

With a savage snort of rage, the beast rushed at this new target—rushed so swiftly and from so short a distance that Marian could not defend herself. She sprang to one side as it charged down upon her, but a glancing blow from its antlers stretched her upon the ground. The stag stopped, turned, and lowered its head, preparing to gore her to death.

Already its cruel horns were coming straight for her, while she, bewildered, was struggling to rise. A moment more and the end would come. But the sharp voice of Robin had already spoken.

"Down, Marian!" he cried, and the girl instinctively obeyed, just as the shaft from Robin's bow went whizzing close above her head and struck with terrific force full in the center of the stag's forehead.

The beast stumbled and fell dead, across Marian's body. She had fainted.

Robin was quickly by her side and dragged the beast off the girl. Picking her up in his strong arms he carried her swiftly to the side of one of the brooks which watered the vale.

He dashed cool water upon her face, roughly almost, in his agony of fear that she was already dead, and he nearly shed tears of joy to see those poor, closed eyelids tremble. Presently she gave a little gasp.

"Where am I? What is it?"

"You are in Sherwood."

She opened her eyes and sat up. "You have rescued me from sudden danger, sir," she said.

Then she recognised Robin for the first time and a radiant smile came over her face. Her head sank upon his shoulder with a little tremble and sigh of relief.

"Oh, Robin, it is you!" she murmured.

"Aye. Thank Heaven, I was at hand to do you service!" Robin's tones were full of feeling. "I swear, dear Marian, that I will not let you from my care again."

Not another word was spoken for some moments, while her head still rested upon his chest. Then recollecting, he suddenly cried:

"Mercy, I make a poor nurse! I have not even asked if any of your bones are broken."

"No," she answered, springing lightly to her feet to show him. "That foolish dizziness overcame me for the moment, but we can now go on our way."

"No, I did not mean that," he protested. "Why should we hurry? First tell me the news in London and of yourself."

So she told him that the Prince had seized her father's lands and promised to restore them to her if she would listen to his proposal, and how she knew that he meant her no good, for he was even then asking for a Princess's hand.

"That is all, Robin," she ended simply, "and that is why I put on my page's costume and came to you."

Robin's brow had grown fiercely black at the recital of her wrongs, and he had laid his hand sternly on the hilt of his sword.

"By this sword that Queen Eleanor gave me!" he said impetuously, "and which is devoted to the service of all women, I promise that Prince John and all his armies shall not harm you!"

So that is how Maid Marian came to live in the greenwood, where the whole band of yeomen welcomed her gladly and Allan-a-Dale's wife made her fully at home.

But this was a day of deeds in Sherwood Forest that led to later events. While Robin and Marian were having their encounter with the stag, Little John, Much the miller's son, and Will Scarlet had gone to watch the high road leading to Barnesdale, on the chance they might meet a knight or priest whose wallet was too full.

They had scarcely watched the great road for many minutes, when they spied a knight riding by in a very sad manner.

Little John came up to the knight and asked him to stop, for who can judge a man's wealth by his looks? The outlaw bent his knee in courtesy and asked the knight to accept the hospitality of the forest.

"My master expects you to dine with him today," he said.

"Who is your master?" asked the knight.

"Robin Hood," replied Little John, laying his hand upon the knight's bridle.

Seeing the other two outlaws approaching, the knight shrugged his shoulders and replied carelessly.

"It is clear that your invitation cannot be refused," said he, "and I go with you right willingly, my friends. My purpose was to dine today at Doncaster, but nothing matters greatly."

So in the same lackadaisical fashion that had marked all his actions that day, the knight let his horse be led to the band's hideaway in the greenwood.

Marian had not yet had time to change her page's costume when the three escorts of the knight came in sight. She recognized their captive as Sir Richard of the Lea, whom she had often seen at court

Little John stops a Sorrowful Knight

and, fearing he might recognize her, she turned to leave. But Robin asked her, with a twinkle, if she would not like to play page, and she consented to do so.

"Welcome, Sir Knight," said Robin courteously. "You are come in good time, for we were just preparing to sit down to eat."

"God save you, Master Robin," returned the knight, "and all your company."

So while his horse was cared for, the knight laid aside his heavy gear, washed his face and hands, and sat down with Robin and all his men to a plentiful dinner of venison, swans, pheasants, various small birds, cakes, and ale. Marian stood behind Robin and filled his cup and that of the guest.

After eating heartily, the knight brightened up greatly and vowed that he had not enjoyed so good a dinner for nearly three weeks. He also said that if ever Robin and his fellows should come to his lands, he would set them down to as good a dinner.

But this was not exactly the sort of payment that Robin expected. He thanked the knight, but reminded him that a yeoman like himself could hardly offer such a dinner to a knight as a gift of charity.

"I have no money, Master Robin," answered the knight frankly. "I have so little of the world's goods, in truth, that I should be ashamed to offer you the whole of it."

"Money, however little, always jingles merrily in our pockets," said Robin, smiling. "Pray, tell me what you consider a little sum."

"I have ten silver pennies," said the knight. "Here they are, and I wish they were ten times as many."

He handed Little John his pouch, and Robin nodded carelessly.

"What is the total, Little John?" he asked.

"It's true enough, as the knight has said," responded the big fellow, emptying the contents on his cloak.

Robin signed to Marian, who filled a cup of wine for himself and his guest.

"Sir Knight!" cried the merry outlaw, "why these sorry times? I see that your armor is bent and that your clothes are torn. Yet I think I saw you at court, once upon a day, and looking more prosperous. Tell me now, have you been a bad steward to yourself and wasted your money in lawsuits and the like? Do not be bashful with us. We shall not betray your secrets."

"I am a Saxon knight in my own right, and I have always lived a sober and quiet life," the sorrowful guest replied. "'Tis true you may have seen me at court, for I saw you at King Harry's tournament. My name is Sir Richard of the Lea, and I dwell in a castle, not far from one of the gates of Nottingham, which has belonged to my father, and his father, and his father's father before him. Two or three years ago my neighbors might have told you that a matter of four hundred pounds one way or the other was nothing to me. But now I have only these ten pennies of silver, and my wife and son."

"How have you lost your riches?" asked Robin.

"Through folly and kindness," said the knight, sighing. "I went with King Richard upon a Crusade, from which I lately returned, in time to find my son grown up. He had achieved a squire's training and could play prettily in jousts and tournaments and other knightly games. But he had the ill luck to accidentally kill a knight in the open lists. To save the boy, I had to sell my lands and mortgage my family's castle, and, this not being enough, in the end I have had to borrow money, at a very high interest, from my lord of Hereford."

"A most worthy Bishop," said Robin. "How much is your debt?"

"Four hundred pounds," said Sir Richard, "and the Bishop swears he will take my castle if they are not paid promptly."

"Have you any friends who would guarantee your promise for you?"

"Not one. If good King Richard were here, the tale might be otherwise."

"Fill your goblet again, Sir Knight," said Robin, and he turned to whisper a word in Marian's ear. She nodded, drew Little John and Will Scarlet aside, and talked earnestly with them, in a low tone.

"Here is health and prosperity to you, gallant Robin," said Sir Richard, tilting his goblet. "I hope I may repay your hospitality more worthily the next time I ride by."

Will Scarlet and Little John meanwhile consulted the other outlaws, who nodded their heads. Then Little John and Will Scarlet went into the cave near by and presently returned bearing a bag of gold. Then they counted out four hundred gold pieces before the astonished knight.

Sir·Richard·pleadeth·before·the·Bishop

"Take this loan from us, Sir Knight, and pay your debt to the Bishop," said Robin. "And you owe us no thanks. You are only exchanging creditors. Perhaps we shall not be so hard upon you as the Christian Bishop. Yet, again, we may be harder. Who can tell?"

There were actual tears in Sir Richard's eyes as he tried to thank the foresters. "God save you, comrades, and keep you all!" said he, with deep feeling. "And give me a grateful heart!"

"We shall wait for you twelve months from today, here in this place," said Robin, shaking him by the hand, "and then you will repay us the loan if you have prospered."

"I shall return it to you within the year, upon my honor as Sir Richard of the Lea. And for all time, count on me as a steadfast friend."

So saying, the knight, led by one of Robin's men, rode down the glade till they were lost to view.

CHAPTER 15

How the Bishop Dined

"'O what is the matter?' then said the Bishop,
  'Or for whom do ye make this ado?'
Or why do ye kill the King's venison,
  When your company is so few?'

"'We are shepherds,' quoth bold Robin Hood,
  'And we keep sheep all the year,
And we are disposed to be merrie this day,
  And to kill of the King's fat deer.'"

NOT MANY DAYS AFTER Sir Richard of the Lea came to Sherwood Forest, word reached Robin Hood that the Bishop of Hereford would be riding that way on that morning. Robin's face brightened as he heard it.

"Now, by our Lady!" he said. "I have long desired to entertain the bishop in the greenwood, and this is too good a chance to let slip. Come, men, kill me a good fat deer. The Bishop of Hereford shall dine with me today and pay well for his dinner."

"Shall we butcher it here as usual?" asked Much, the miller's son.

"No. We will play a game on the churchman. We will dress it by the highway side and watch for the Bishop closely, in case he should ride some other way."

So Robin gave his orders, and most of his men went to different parts of the forest, under Will Stutely and Little John, to watch other roads. Robin Hood took six of his men, including Will Scarlet and Much, and placed himself in full view on the main road. This little company disguised themselves as shepherds. Robin had an old wool cap, with a tail to it, hanging over his ear, and a shock of hair stood straight up through a hole in the top. Besides, there was so much dirt on his face that you would never have known him. An old tattered cloak over his hunter's garb completed his makeup. The others were no less ragged and filthy.

They quickly shot themselves a deer and were preparing to cook it over a small fire, when a little dust was seen blowing along the highway and out of it came the portly Bishop, cantering along, with ten men-at-arms at his heels. As soon as he saw the shepherds he spurred up his horse and came straight toward them.

"Who are you to make so free with the King's deer?" he asked sharply.

"We are shepherds," answered Robin Hood, pulling at his cap awkwardly.

"Heaven have mercy! You seem a sorry lot. Who gave you permission to stop eating mutton?"

"It's one of our feast days, and we wish to be merry and dine on deer, out here where they are so many."

"The King shall hear of this. Who killed yon beast?"

"First give me your name, your excellence, so that I may speak as is fitting," replied Robin stubbornly.

"It's my lord Bishop of Hereford, fellow!" interjected one of the guards fiercely. "See that you keep a civil tongue in your head."

"If he is a churchman," retorted Will Scarlet, "he would do better to mind his own flocks rather than concern himself with ours."

"You are sassy fellows," cried the Bishop. "And we will see if your heads will pay for your manners. Quit your stolen roast and march along with me, for you shall be brought before the Sheriff of Nottingham immediately."

"Pardon, your excellence!" said Robin, dropping on his knees. "Pardon, I pray you. It does not become your calling to take so many lives away."

"I'll pardon you when I see you hanged!" said the Bishop. "Seize them, men!"

But Robin had already sprung away. And from underneath his ragged cloak he drew his trusty horn and blew those piercing notes that summoned the band.

The Bishop no sooner saw this action than he knew that Robin had set a trap. Being a coward, he wheeled his horse sharply and would have ridden off down the road, but his own men blocked his way. At almost the same instant the bushes around seemed to come alive with outlaws. Little John's men came from one side and Will Stutely's from the other. The worthy Bishop soon found himself a prisoner and began to beg mercy from the men he had so lately been ready to hang.

"O pardon, O pardon, I pray you," said the Bishop. "For if I had known it was you, I'd have gone some other way.'"

"I owe you nothing," retorted Robin. "I will even treat you better than you would have treated me. Come along with me. I have already planned for you to dine with me this day."

So the unwilling bishop was dragged away, with the half-cooked venison upon the back of his own horse; and Robin and his band took charge of the whole company and led them through the forest till they came to an open space near Barnesdale.

Here they rested. Much, the miller's son, began roasting the deer again, while another and fatter beast was set to sizzle on the other side of the fire. Presently the appetizing odor of the cooking reached the Bishop's nostrils, and he sniffed it eagerly. The morning's ride had made him hungry, and he did not hesitate when they called him to dinner. Robin gave him the place beside himself, and the Bishop prepared to eat.

"Nay, my lord, but we are accustomed to say grace before eating," said Robin. "And as our own chaplain is not with us today, will you be good enough to say it for us?"

The Bishop reddened, but pronounced grace in Latin hastily and then settled himself to make the best of his lot. Red wines and ale were poured out into their horn tankards.

Laughter bubbled among the diners, and the Bishop caught himself smiling at more than one jest. But who could resist a freshly broiled venison steak eaten out in the open air to the tune of good fellowship? Stutely filled the Bishop's tankard with wine each time he emptied it, and the Bishop got mellower and mellower as the afternoon shadows lengthened on towards sunset. Then the approaching dusk warned him of his position.

"I wish," said he gravely to Robin, who had soberly drunk only one cup of ale, "that you would tell me what I owe you. 'Tis late, and I fear the cost of this entertainment may be more than my poor purse can stand."

"Indeed, your lordship," said Robin, scratching his head, "I have enjoyed your company so much that I scarcely know how to charge for it."

"Lend me your purse, my lord," said Little John, interposing, "and I'll give you the reckoning by and by."

The Bishop shuddered. He had collected Sir Richard's debt that very morning and was even then carrying it home.

"I have but a few silver pennies of my own," he whined. "And as for the gold in my saddlebags, it is for the church. Surely you would not take from the church, good friends."

But Little John had already gone to the saddlebags, and when he returned he laid the Bishop's cloak on the ground and poured out four hundred glittering gold pieces. It was the identical money Robin lent Sir Richard a short while before!

"Ah!" said Robin, as though an idea had but just then come to him. "The church is always willing to aid in charity. And seeing this goodly sum reminds me that I have a friend who is indebted to a churchman for this exact amount. Now, we shall charge you nothing for your dinner, but we'll make use of this to aid my good friend."

"No, no," began the Bishop, with a worried look. "Was this not the King's meat, after all, that we feasted upon? Furthermore, I am a poor man."

"Poor!" answered Robin in scorn. "You are the Bishop of Hereford. Does not the whole countryside speak of your cruelty to the poor and ignorant—you who should use your great office to aid instead of oppress them? Have you not been guilty of far greater robbery than this, even though less open? Of myself, I say nothing, nor of your unjust hatred against my father. But on account of those you have robbed and oppressed I take this money, and I will use it to a far more worthy purpose than you would. God be my witness in this! There is an end of the matter, unless you will lead us in a song or dance to show that your body has a better spirit than your mind. Strike up the harp, Allan!"

"Neither will I do," snarled the Bishop.

"Then we must help you," said Little John, and he seized the fat, struggling churchman and began to hop up and down. The Bishop, being shorter, was forced to dance, while the whole company sat and rolled about over the ground and roared. At last he sank in a heap, fuddled with wine and quite exhausted.

Little John picked him up as though he were a log of wood and, carrying him to his horse, set him on it facing the animal's tail. Then leading the animal toward the high road, he sent the Bishop, more dead than alive, toward Nottingham.

CHAPTER 16

How the Sheriff Held Another Shooting Match

"To tell the truth, I'm well informed
Yon match 'tis a wile;
*The Sheriff, I **wis**, devises this*
Us archers to beguile."

T HE SHERIFF WAS SO GREATLY troubled over the growing power of Robin Hood that he did a very foolish thing. He went to London to lay his troubles before the King and get more troops to cope with the outlaws. King Richard was not yet returned from the Holy Land, but Prince John heard him with scorn.

"Pooh!" said he, shrugging his shoulders. "What have I to do with all this? Are you not

WIS
Know.

sheriff for me? The law is in force that lets you deal with those who injure you. Go, get gone, and by yourself devise some trick to trap these rebels. And never let me see your face at court again until you have a better tale to tell."

So away the Sheriff went sorrier than ever and beat his brain on the way home for some plan of action.

His daughter met him on his return, and when she learned what the Prince had said, his words started her thinking.

"I have it!" she exclaimed at length. "We will hold another shooting match! We will proclaim a general amnesty, as King Harry himself did, and say that the field is open to all comers. Robin Hood's men will be tempted to twang the bow, and then—"

"And then," said the Sheriff, jumping up, "we shall see on which side of the gate they stay overnight!"

So the Sheriff lost no time in announcing a tournament, to be held that autumn at the Fair. It was open to all comers, said the proclamation, and no one would be molested in their going and coming. Furthermore, an arrow with a golden head and silver shaft would be given to the winner, who would be named the finest archer in all the North Country.

The·Sheriff·of·Nottingham·cometh·
before·the·King·at·London

This news came in due course to Robin Hood and fired his impetuous spirit.

"Prepare you, my merry men," said he, "and we'll go to the Fair and take part in this sport."

With that the cobbler, David of Doncaster, stepped forward.

"Master," said he, "do not leave the forest. To tell the truth, I'm well informed that the match is a trap. The Sheriff has planned it to lead us into treachery."

"That sounds cowardly," replied Robin, "and pleases me not. Let come what will, I'll try my skill at the tourney."

Then Little John spoke up: "Listen to me how it shall be that we will not be discovered. We will leave our suits of Lincoln green behind us. One shall wear white, another red, one yellow, another blue, and thus all shall go in disguise."

This advice met with general favor and Maid Marian and Mistress Dale, assisted by Friar Tuck, prepared some colored costumes and fitted out the men so that others would take them for villagers dressed for the holiday.

And on the Fair day they left the greenwood with

brave hearts. Along the highway they fell in with many other fellows from the countryside, going with their lasses toward the wide-open gates of Nottingham.

So in through the gates trooped the whole happy company, Robin's men behaving and laughing and talking as noisily as the rest. The Sheriff's scowling men-at-arms stood about and sought anyone who looked like one of Robin's men, but without success.

The herald now set forth the terms of the contest, and presently the shooting began. Robin had chosen five of his men to shoot with him. The rest were to mingle with the crowd and also watch the gates. These five were Little John, Will Scarlet, Will Stutely, Much, and Allan-a-Dale.

The other competitors made a brave showing on the first round, especially Gilbert of the White Hand, who was present and never shot better. The contest narrowed down until in the end Gilbert and Robin alone were left to shoot for the possession of the arrow with the golden head. The shooting went forward, and Robin's men had done so well that the air was filled with shouts. Thus went the second round of the shooting, and thus the third and last, until even Gilbert of the

White Hand was fairly beaten. During all this shooting, Robin exchanged no word with his men. Each treated the other as a perfect stranger. Nonetheless, such great shooting could not pass without revealing the archers.

The Sheriff believed the winner of the golden arrow to be Robin Hood, so he secretly sent word for his men-at-arms to close round the group. But Robin's men also saw the trap closing.

To keep up appearances, the Sheriff summoned the crowd to form a circle—to give time enough for the soldiers to close in—and after as much delay as possible, the arrow was presented. As Robin received his prize, bowed and turned away, the Sheriff grasped him about the neck and called upon his men to arrest him.

But the moment the Sheriff touched Robin, he received such a blow on the side of his head that he let go instantly and fell back several paces. Turning to see who had struck him, he recognized Little John.

By this time fighting broke out everywhere. The Sheriff's men were being hampered by the crowd of inno- cent onlookers, whom they could not tell from the out- laws, and so dared not attack. Meanwhile the other out- laws in the rear fell upon them and put them in confusion.

For a moment the Sheriff's men took a beating. Then with a clear bugle note, Robin ordered a retreat. The two guards at the nearest gate tried to close it, but were shot dead in their tracks. David of Doncaster threw a third soldier into the moat, and out through the gate went the foresters in good order, keeping a safe distance between themselves and the soldiers by means of their well-aimed arrows.

But the fight was not to go easily this day. The soldiers, knowing that the eyes of the whole shire were upon them, fought well and pressed closely after the retreating outlaws. More than one ugly wound was given and received. Five of the Sheriff's men were killed outright and a dozen others injured. Four of Robin's men were bleeding from severe cuts.

Then Little John, who had fought by the side of his chief, suddenly fell forward with a moan. An arrow had pierced his knee. Robin seized the big fellow with almost superhuman strength, took him on his back and carried him more than a mile.

Meanwhile Little John grew weaker and closed his eyes. At last he sank to the ground and feebly motioned Robin to let him lie.

"Master Robin," said he, "have I not served you well ever since we met upon the bridge?"

"A truer friend a man never had," answered Robin.

"Then if ever you loved me, and for the sake of that friendship, draw your bright sword and strike off my head. Never let me fall alive into the hands of the Sheriff of Nottingham."

"Not for all the gold in England would I do either of the things you suggest."

"God forbid!" cried Arthur-a-Bland, who was Little John's cousin, as he hurried to the rescue. And, packing his wounded kinsman upon his own broad shoulders, he soon brought him within the shelter of the forest.

Once they were there, the Sheriff's men did not follow. Little John and the other four wounded men were quickly carried through the wood to Friar Tuck's hermitage, where their wounds were dressed. Little John's injury was the most serious of any, but he was assured that in two or three weeks' time he could get about again, news which caused the active giant to groan mightily.

That evening fear came upon the hearts of the

band. A careful roll call was taken to see if all the yeomen had escaped. Will Stutely was missing, and Maid Marian also was nowhere to be found. Robin was gripped with dread. He knew that Marian had gone to the Fair. Her absence meant danger to her, and he feared that it was connected with Will Stutely. The Sheriff would hang him speedily, and without mercy, if he were captured.

The rest of the band knew that if Will were captured, the battle must be fought over again the next day and Will must be saved at any cost. But no man flinched from the danger.

That evening, while the Sheriff and his wife and daughter sat at supper in the Mansion House, the Sheriff boasted of how he would make an example of the captured outlaw, for Stutely had indeed fallen into his hands.

"He shall be strung high," he said in a loud voice, "and none shall dare lift a finger. I now have Robin Hood's men on the run, and we shall soon see who is master in this shire. I am only sorry that we let them have the golden arrow."

As he spoke a message sped through a window and fell clattering upon his plate, causing him to spring back in alarm.

It was the golden arrow, and on its shaft a little note was tied. It read:

"I will take no gifts from liars and from now on will show you no mercy. Look well to yourself.   R.H."

CHAPTER 17

How Will Stutely
Was Rescued

"Forth of the greenwood are they gone,
Yea, all courageously,
Resolving to bring Stutely home,
Or every man to die."

THE NEXT DAY DAWNED bright and sunny. All of
nature seemed happy, despite the tragedy that
was soon to take place within the walls of
Nottingham. The Sheriff was determined to hang Will
Stutely. No man, therefore, was to be allowed through
the town's gates until after the fatal hour of noon, when
Will's soul was to be launched into eternity.

Early in the day Robin had drawn his men to a
point in the woods where he could watch the road lead-

ing to the east gate. He was clad in a bright scarlet tunic, while his men wore their suits of Lincoln green. They were armed with broadswords, and each man carried his bow and a full quiver of new arrows, straightened and sharpened keenly. Over their greenwood dress, each man had thrown a rough cloak that made him look like a friar.

"Comrades," said Robin Hood then, "we'll wait here in hiding while we send someone forth to obtain tidings. It will do no good to march upon the gates if they are closed."

"Look, master," said David of Doncaster. "There comes a **palmer** along the road from the town. Perhaps he can tell us how the land lies, and if Stutely is really in danger. Shall I speak to him?"

"Go," answered Robin.

So David of Doncaster went out, and when he had come close to the palmer, who seemed a slight, youngish man, he lifted his cap courteously and said:

PALMER
A person who made a pilgrimage to the Holy Land. They often wore two crossed palm leaves as a sign of their journey.

"I beg your pardon, holy man, but can you tell me news of Nottingham?

The · Aged · Palmer · gives · Yovng · David · of · Doncaster · news · of · Will · Stvtely

Do they intend to put an outlaw to death this day?"

"Aye," answered the palmer sadly. "'Tis true enough, sorry be the day. I have passed the very spot where the gallowstree is going up, out upon the roadway near the Sheriff's castle. Will Stutely is to be hung at noon, and I could not bear the sight, so I came away."

The palmer spoke in a muffled voice, as his hood was pulled well over his head. He carried a long staff and he had sandalled feet like any monk. David of Doncaster noticed idly that the feet were very small and white, but gave no second thought to the matter.

"Who will hear the poor soul's last confession if you have left him?" he asked angrily.

The question seemed to put a new idea into the palmer's head. He turned so quickly that he almost dropped his hood.

"Do you think that I should do this holy office?"

"By Saint Peter and the Blessed Virgin, I do indeed! Else, who will do it? The Bishop may be there, but he would not say a prayer for Will's soul."

"But I am only a poor palmer," the other began hesitatingly.

"But your prayers are as good as any and better

than some," replied David.

"Right gladly would I go," said the palmer then. "But I fear I cannot get into the city. The gates are locked to all who wish to come in, although they let anyone pass out who will."

"Come with me," said David, "and my master will see that you pass through the gates."

So the palmer pulled his cloak still closer about him and was brought before Robin Hood, to whom he told all he knew of the situation. He ended with:

"If I may make so bold, I would not try to enter the city from this gate. 'Tis closely guarded since yesterday. But on the far side, no attack is looked for."

"My thanks, gentle palmer," said Robin; "your suggestion is good, and we will go to the gate on the far side."

So the men marched silently but quickly until they were near the western gate. Then Arthur-a-Bland asked leave to go ahead as a scout and quietly made his way to a point under the tower by the gate. The moat was dry on this side, as this was a time of peace, and Arthur was further aided by a stout ivy vine which grew out from an upper window.

Swinging himself up boldly by means of this friendly vine, he crept through the window and sprung upon the guard from behind and gripped him hard about the throat. The guard had no chance to utter the slightest sound and soon lay bound and gagged upon the floor, while Arthur-a-Bland changed into his uniform and got hold of his keys.

In a few moments more the gates were open, the drawbridge let down, and the rest of the band got inside the town so quietly that no one knew of their coming. Fortune also favored them in the fact that just at this moment the prison doors opened for the march of the condemned man, and every soldier in the marketplace had trooped there to see him pass by.

Out came Will Stutely with firm steps but a dejected air. He looked eagerly to the right and left, but saw none of the band. And though more than one curious face showed friendship in it, he knew no help could come from them.

Will's hands were tied behind his back. He marched between rows of soldiers, and the Sheriff and the Bishop brought up the rear on horses, looking puffed up over their success. He would show these sturdy rebels—would the Sheriff—whose word was law! He knew that the gates were tightly fastened, and further he believed that the outlaws would hardly dare to come within the walls again, even if the gates were open. And as he looked around at the hundred archers and swordsmen who lined the way to the gallows, he smiled with grim satisfaction.

Seeing that no help was near, the prisoner paused at the foot of the scaffold and spoke in a firm tone to the Sheriff.

"My lord Sheriff," said he, "since I must die, grant me one request: Give me a sword and let me fight till I lie dead on the ground."

But instead the Sheriff swore that Will should be hanged, a shameful death, and not die valiantly.

"To the gallows with him!" he roared, giving a sign to the hangman. Stutely was pushed into the cart which was to hold him under the gallows while his neck was leashed. Then the cart would be drawn away and the unhappy man would swing out over the tail of it into another world.

But at this moment came an interruption. A boyish-looking palmer stepped forth and said:

"Your Excellency, let me at least **shrive** this poor wretch's soul before it is hurled into eternity."

"No!" shouted the Sheriff, "let him die a dog's death!"

SHRIVE
To listen to someone confessing his sins.

"Then his damnation will rest upon you," said the monk firmly. "You, my lord Bishop, cannot stand by and see this wrong done."

The Bishop hesitated. Like the Sheriff, he wanted no delay; but the people were beginning to mutter among themselves and move about uneasily. He said a few words to the Sheriff, and the latter nodded to the monk coldly.

"Perform your duty," he said. "And be quick about it!" Then turning to his soldiers, he commanded, "Watch this palmer closely. He may be in league with those rascally outlaws."

But the palmer paid no heed to his last words. He began to **tell his beads** quickly and to speak in a low voice to the condemned man. But he did not touch the ropes binding his hands.

TELL HIS BEADS
To pray the rosary, a string of beads used in praying about virtues in the lives of Jesus and Mary.

Then came another stir in the crowd as one man came pushing through the press of people and soldiers to come near the scaffold.

"I pray you, Will, before you die, say goodbye to all your friends!" cried out the well-known voice of Much, the miller's son.

At these words, the palmer stepped back suddenly and looked to one side. The Sheriff also knew the speaker.

"Seize him!" he shouted. "He is the villain cook who once robbed me of my silver plate. We'll make a double hanging of this!"

"Not so fast, Sheriff," retorted Much. "First catch your man, then hang him. But meanwhile I would like to borrow my friend awhile."

And with one stroke of his keen hunting knife he cut the bonds that fastened the prisoner's arms, and Stutely leaped lightly from the cart.

"Treason!" screamed the Sheriff, getting black with rage.

So saying he spurred his horse fiercely forward and, rising in his stirrups, brought down his sword powerfully at Much's head. But his former cook dodged nimbly underneath the horse and came up on the other side, while the weapon whistled harmlessly in the air.

"Nay, Sir Sheriff!" he cried, " I must borrow your sword for my friend."

Then he snatched the weapon deftly from the Sheriff's hand.

"Here, Stutely!" said he, "the Sheriff has lent you his own sword. Get back to back with me, man, and we'll teach these knaves a trick or two!"

Meanwhile the soldiers had recovered from their momentary surprise and had flung themselves into the fray. A clear bugle note had also sounded—the one that the soldiers had learned to dread. It was the rallying note of Robin's men. Arrows began to hurtle through the air, and Robin and his men cast aside their cloaks and sprang forward crying:

"Lockesley! Lockesley! A rescue! A rescue!"

Terrible hand-to-hand fighting followed. The Sheriff's men, though once more taken by surprise, were determined to prevent the rescue at all costs. They packed in stubbornly around the condemned man and Much and the palmer, and it was only by desperate attacks that the foresters made an opening in the square.

Ugly cuts and bruises were exchanged freely, and lucky was the man who escaped with only these. Many of the onlookers, who had long hated the Sheriff and felt sympathy for Robin's men, also plunged into the conflict and aided the rescuers.

At last, Robin cut a way through the fighting to the scaffold itself, and not a second too soon. Two soldiers had leaped upon the cart and were about to stab the palmer and Will Stutely. A mighty upward blow from Robin's blade sent the sword flying from the hand of one, while a well-directed arrow from the outskirts pierced the other fellow's throat.

"God save you, master!" cried Will Stutely joyfully. "I had begun to fear that I would never see your face again."

"A rescue!" shouted the outlaws afresh, and the soldiers began to sink back. But they retreated in close order toward the east gate, resolved to hem the attackers within the city walls. But the outlaws did not go out by their nearest gate. They started heading in that direction, in order to mislead the soldiers, then abruptly turned and headed for the west gate, which was still guarded by Arthur-a-Bland.

The Sheriff's men raised a shout at this, thinking they had the enemy trapped. They charged after them, but the outlaws soon got through the gate and over the bridge that had been let down by Arthur-a-Bland.

Close upon their heels came the soldiers—so close that Arthur had no time to close the gate again or raise the bridge. So he threw away his key and joined with the yeomen in their retreat up the long hill to the woods.

On this side of the town, the road leading to the forest was long and open. The greenwood men were therefore in some distress, for the archers shot at them from loopholes in the walls, and the soldiers were reinforced by a company of mounted men from the castle. But the outlaws retreated stubbornly and now and again turned to hold their pursuers at bay by a volley of arrows. Stutely was in their midst, fighting with the energy of two; and the little palmer was there also but took no part except to keep close to Robin's side and mutter silent words as though in prayer.

Robin put his horn to his lips to sound a rally, when a flying arrow from the enemy pierced his hand. The palmer gave a little cry and sprang forward. The

Sheriff, who followed close with his men on horseback, also saw the wound and gave a great hurrah.

"Ha! you will shoot no more bows for a season, master outlaw!" he shouted.

"You lie!" retorted Robin fiercely, wrenching the shaft from his hand despite the streaming blood. "I have saved one shot for you all this day. Here take it!"

And he fitted the same arrow that had wounded him upon the string of his bow and let it fly toward the Sheriff's head. The Sheriff fell forward upon his horse in mortal terror, but not quickly enough to escape unhurt. The sharp point cut a deep gash across his scalp and would certainly have killed him if it had come closer.

The Sheriff's fall confused his followers for the moment and Robin's men took this chance to speed on up the hill. The palmer had whipped out a small white handkerchief and tried to staunch Robin's wound as they went. At sight of the palmer's hand, Robin turned and pushed back the other's hood.

"Marian!" he exclaimed, "You—here?"

It was indeed Maid Marian, who had helped save Will and been in the battle from the first. Now she hung her head as though caught doing wrong.

"I had to come, Robin," she said simply, "and I knew you would not let me otherwise."

Their talk was interrupted by an exclamation from Will Scarlet.

"By the saints, we are trapped!" he said, and pointed to the top of the hill, toward which they were moving.

From out of a grey castle poured a troop of men, armed with pikes and axes, who shouted and came running down upon them. At the same instant, the Sheriff's men also renewed their pursuit.

"Alas!" cried poor Marian, "we are doomed! There is no way of escape!"

"Courage, dear heart!" said Robin, drawing her close to him. But his own spirit sank as he looked about for some way out.

Then—oh joyful sight!— he recognized at the head of those coming from the castle Sir Richard of the Lea. He was smiling now and greatly excited.

"A rescue! A rescue!" he cried.

Never were there more welcome sights and sounds than these. With a great cheer the outlaws raced up the hill to meet their new friends; soon the whole force was inside the shelter of the castle. Bang! went the bridge as it swung back up, with great clanking of chains. Clash! went one heavy door upon the other as they shut out the Sheriff, who dashed up at the head of his men, his face streaked with blood and inflamed with rage.

CHAPTER 18

How Sir Richard of the Lea Repaid His Debt

"The proud Sheriff loud 'gan cry
And said, 'Thou traitor knight,
Thou keepest here the King's enemy
Against the laws and right.'"

"OPEN THE GATES!" shouted the Sheriff hoarsely to the sentinel upon the walls. "Open, I say, in the King's name!"

"Who are you to come brawling upon my land?" asked Sir Richard, who himself stepped forward upon the turret.

"You know me well, traitor!" said the Sheriff. "Now give up the enemy of the King whom you have sheltered against the laws."

"Softly, sir," said the knight smoothly. "I confess that I have done certain deeds this day. But I have done them upon mine own land, which you now trespass upon; and I shall answer only to the King for my actions."

"Villain!" said the Sheriff, still in a towering passion. "I, also, serve the King; if these outlaws are not given up to me at once, I shall lay seige to the castle and burn it."

"First show me your warrants," said Sir Richard curtly.

"My word is enough! I am Sheriff of Nottingham!"

"If you are," retorted the knight, "you should know that you have no authority within my lands unless you bear the King's order. In the meantime, go mend your manners."

And Sir Richard disappeared from the walls. The Sheriff, after lingering a few moments longer, was forced to withdraw, muttering fiercely:

"The King's order! That I shall have without delay, as well as this upstart knight's estates. King Richard is lately returned, I hear, from the Holy Land."

Meanwhile the knight had gone back to Robin Hood, and the two men greeted each other gladly.

"Well, bold Robin!" cried he, taking him in his arms. "The Lord has lately prospered me, and I saw this day how I could repay my debt to you."

"And so you have," answered Robin gaily.

"Nay, 'twas nothing—a small service!" said the knight. "I meant the money coming to you."

"But it has all been repaid," said Robin. "My lord Bishop of Hereford himself gave it to me."

"The exact sum?" asked the knight.

"The exact sum," answered Robin, winking.

Sir Richard smiled but said no more. Robin was made to rest until dinner should be served. Meanwhile a surgeon bound up his hand with ointment, promising him that he would soon be able to use it again. Ten other yeomen had been hurt, but luckily none had received serious wounds. They were all bandaged and made happy by tankards of ale.

The feast was a joyous event. There were two long tables, and two hundred men sat down at them and ate and drank and afterward sang songs. A hundred and forty of these men wore Lincoln green and called Robin

Hood their chief. Never had there been a more gallant company at the table in Lea Castle!

That night the foresters stayed within the friendly walls, and the next day they took their leave. Sir Richard took Robin aside to his strong room and pressed him again to take the four hundred golden pounds. But his guest was firm.

"Keep the money, for it is your own," said Robin. "I only made the Bishop return that which he took unjustly."

Sir Richard thanked him earnestly and asked him and all his men to visit the armory, before they departed. There they saw, placed apart, a hundred and forty good yew bows with fine waxen silk strings and a hundred and forty sheaves of arrows. Every shaft was set with peacocks' feathers and notched with silver.

"In truth, these are poor presents we have made you, Robin Hood," said Sir Richard. "But they carry with them a thousand times their weight in gratitude."

THE SHERIFF MADE GOOD his threat to inform the King. He rode to London the week following, his scalp wound having healed well enough to permit him to travel. He asked for an audience with King Richard the Lion Hearted himself. His Majesty had but lately returned from the Crusades and was just then looking into the state of his kingdom.

The Sheriff spoke at length concerning Robin Hood; how for many months the outlaws had defied the King and slain the King's deer; how Robin had gathered about him the best archers in all the countryside; and, finally, how the traitorous knight Sir Richard of the Lea had rescued the band when capture seemed certain and refused to deliver them up to justice.

The King heard him through with attention, and said he:

"I have heard of this Robin Hood and his men. Did not these same outlaws shoot in a royal tourney at Finsbury Field?"

"They did, Your Majesty, under a royal amnesty."

"And did they come to the Fair at Nottingham by stealth?"

"Yes, Your Majesty."

"Did you forbid them to come?"

"No, Your Majesty. That is—"

"Speak out!"

"For the good of the shire," began the Sheriff, falteringly, "we proclaimed an amnesty, declaring that all men could come safely. But it was because these men had proved a menace that this trap was set."

"Now!" said the King, as his brow grew black. "Such treachery would be unknown in the camp of the **Saracen**, and yet we call ourselves a Christian people!"

The Sheriff kept silent from fear and shame. Then the King spoke again:

"My lord Sheriff, we promise to look into this matter. Those outlaws must be taught that there is only one King in England, and that he stands for the law."

So the Sheriff was dismissed, with very mixed feelings, and went home to Nottingham.

SARACEN
Arabs who fought the Christians in the Crusades.

A **FORTNIGHT** LATER THE KING BEGAN to make good his word, by riding with a small party of knights to Lea Castle. Sir Richard was advised of the cavalcade's approach and quickly recognized the tall knight who rode in front as his royal master. Opening wide his castle gate, he went to meet

FORTNIGHT
Two weeks.

the King and fell on one knee and kissed his stirrup. Sir Richard had been with the King in the Holy Land, and they had gone on many adventurous quests together.

The King dismounted from his own horse to greet him as a brother-in-arms, and arm-in-arm they went into the castle, while bugles and trumpets sounded a joyous welcome in honor of the great occasion.

After the King had rested and eaten, he turned to the knight and gravely inquired:

"What is this I hear about your castle being a nest and harbor for outlaws?"

Then Sir Richard of the Lea, perceiving that the Sheriff had been at the King's ear with his story, told the whole truth as he knew it: how the outlaws had befriended him in sore need—as they had befriended others—and how he had given them only a knight's protection in return.

The King liked the story well, for his own soul was one of **chivalry**. And he asked other questions about Robin Hood, and heard of the ancient wrong done to his father before him, and of Robin's own enemies, and of his manner of living.

CHIVALRY
The ideals of medieval knights that emphasized gallantry, honor and courtesy, especially toward women.

"I must see this bold fellow for myself!" cried King Richard, springing up. "If you will entertain my little company and be ready to sally forth, upon the second day, in quest of me if need be, I shall go alone into the greenwood to seek an adventure with him."

CHAPTER 19

How King Richard Came to Sherwood Forest

"King Richard hearing of the pranks
Of Robin Hood and his men,
He much admired and more desired
To see both him and them.
......
"Then Robin takes a can of ale:
'Come let us now begin;
And every man shall have his can;
Here's a health unto the King!'"

FRIAR TUCK NURSED Little John's wounded knee so skillfully that it was now healed. The last part of the nursing consisted chiefly of holding down the patient, by force, to his cot. Little John felt so well that he insisted upon getting up before the wound was healed. He would have done so, if the friar had not piled some holy books upon his legs and sat upon his stomach. Under this vigorous treatment Little John was forced to lie quiet until the friar gave him leave to get up. At last he and the friar went to join the rest of the band, who were very glad to see them. They sat round a big fire, for it was a chilly evening, and feasted in great content.

A cold rain set in later, but the friar made his way back to his little hermitage. There he made himself a cheerful blaze, changed his dripping robe, and sat down with a sigh of satisfaction before a tankard of hot spiced wine and a pastry. Suddenly a voice was heard outside demanding to be let in. His kennel of dogs set up a furious uproar, proving the fact of a stranger's presence.

"Now by Saint Peter!" growled the friar. "Who comes here at this unseemly hour? Move on, friend, or my spiced wine will get cold!"

He was putting the tankard to his lips when a thundering rap sounded upon the door, making it quiver, and causing Tuck almost to drop his tankard. An angry voice shouted:

"Ho! Within there! Open, I say!"

"Go your way in peace!" roared back the friar. "I

can do nothing for you. It's but a few miles to Gamewell, if you know the road."

"But I do not know the road, and if I did I would not budge another foot. It's wet out and dry within. So, open!"

"A plague seize you for disturbing a holy man in his prayers!" muttered Tuck angrily. He unbarred the door in order to keep it from being battered down. Then lighting a torch at his fire and whistling for one of his dogs, he stepped out to see who his visitor might be.

A tall knight clad in a black coat of mail, with a plumed helmet, stood before him. By his side stood his horse, also dressed in rich armor.

"Have you no supper, brother?" asked the Black Knight curtly. "I must beg of you a bed and a bit of roof for tonight, and I wish to refresh my body before I sleep."

"I have no room that even your steed would accept, Sir Knight, and nothing to eat save a crust of bread and a pitcher of water."

"I can smell better food than that, brother, and must force my company upon you, though I shall repay it with gold in the name of the church. As for my horse, let him but be blanketed and put on the sheltered side of the house."

And with that the knight boldly brushed past Tuck and his dog and entered the hermitage. Something about his masterful air pleased Tuck, in spite of his rudeness.

"Sit down, Sir Knight," said he, "and I will fasten up your steed and find him some grain. Half of my bed and board is yours, this night, but we shall see later who is the better man, and who is to give the orders!"

"I can pay my keeping in blows or gold, as you prefer!" said the knight, laughing.

The friar presently returned and drew up a small table near the fire.

"Now, Sir Knight," said he, "put off your sword and helmet and other war gear and help me lay this table, for I am very hungry."

The knight did as he was told and put aside the visor which had hidden his face. He was a bronzed and bearded man with blue eyes and hair shot with gold.

Then once again the priest sat down to his pastry and spiced wine. He said grace with some haste and was surprised to hear his guest respond fittingly in the Latin

tongue. Then they attacked the wine and pastry valiantly. Tuck looked regretfully at the rapidly disappearing
food but did not begrudge it, because of the stories his
guest told to enliven the meal. The wine and warmth of
the room cheered them both, and they
were soon laughing uproariously as
the best of comrades in the world.
The Black Knight, it seemed, had
travelled everywhere. He had been
on Crusades, had fought the noble
Saladin, had been in prison, and often
in peril. But now he spoke of it lightly, laughed it off, and made himself
so friendly that Friar Tuck was nearly choked with merriment. So passed
the time till late, and the two fell asleep
together, one on each side of the table.

SALADIN
Sultan of Egypt
(1137-1193) during the
Third Crusade. He was a
brilliant general and
earned a reputation for
chivalry among his
Christian enemies.

Friar Tuck awoke in a surly mood but was speedily cheered by the sight of the Black Knight, who had
already risen as happy as a lark, washed his face and
hands, and was now stirring hot **gruel** over the fire.

"By my faith, I make a sorry host!" cried
Tuck, springing to his feet. And later as they sat

GRUEL
Thin oatmeal
porridge.

at breakfast, he added: "I do not want your gold. Instead I will do what I can to help you on your way whenever you wish to depart."

"Then tell me," said the knight, "how I may find Robin Hood the outlaw. I have a message to him from the King. All day yesterday I sought him, but found him not."

Friar Tuck lifted up his hands in holy horror. "I am a lover of peace, Sir Knight, and do not keep company with Robin Hood."

"Nay, I mean no harm to Master Hood," said the knight, "but I yearn to speak with him in person."

"If that is all, I can guide you to his hideaway," said Tuck, who foresaw in this knight a possible goldbag for Robin. "In truth, I could not live in these woods without hearing of the outlaws, but matters of religion are my chief joy and occupation."

"I will go with you, brother," said the Black Knight.

So without more ado they went into the forest, the knight riding upon his charger and Tuck pacing along by his side.

The knight sniffed the fresh air in delight.

"The good greenwood is the best place to live in, after all!" said he. "What court or capital can equal this, for true men?"

"None on this earth," replied Tuck smilingly. And once more his heart warmed toward this courteous stranger.

They had not gone more than three or four miles along the road from Fountain Abbey to Barnesdale, when of a sudden the bushes just ahead of them parted and a well-built man with curling brown hair stepped into the road and laid his hand upon the knight's bridle.

It was Robin Hood. He had seen Friar Tuck a little way back and shrewdly suspected his plan. Tuck, however, pretended not to know him at all.

"Hold!" cried Robin. "I am in charge of the highway this day and must exact an accounting from all who pass by."

"Who is it bids me hold?" asked the knight quietly. "I am not in the habit of yielding to one man."

"Then there are others to keep me company," said Robin, clapping his hands. And instantly ten of his men came out of the bushes and stood beside him.

"We are yeomen of the forest, Sir Knight,"

continued Robin, "and live under the greenwood tree. We have no means of support—thanks to the tyranny of our overlords—other than the aid which fat churchmen and goodly knights like yourself can give. And as you have churches and rents and gold in great plenty, we beseech you for charity's sake to give us some."

"I am but a poor monk, good sir!" said Friar Tuck in a whining voice, "on my way to the shrine of **Saint Dunstan.**"

"Stay awhile with us," answered Robin, biting back a smile.

The Black Knight now spoke again. "But we are messengers of the King," said he. "His Majesty himself waits near here and wishes to speak with Robin Hood."

"God save the King!" said Robin, raising his cap loyally. "And all who wish him well! I am Robin Hood, and the

SAINT DUNSTAN
An English saint (910-988), Archbishop of Canterbury and advisor to kings, he revived English monasteries after their destruction by Viking invaders. He was also known for his skill at playing the harp and making bells. According to legend, he once grabbed the devil by the nose with a pair of tongs.

King has no more devoted subject than I. Nor have I taken anything of his save, perhaps, a few deer for my hunger. My chief war is against the clergy and barons of the land who bear down upon the poor. But I am glad," he continued, "that I have met you here; and before we end you shall be my friend and taste of our forest hospitality."

"But what is the fee?" asked the knight. "For I am told your feasts are costly."

"Nay," responded Robin, waving his hands. "You are from the King. Nonetheless, how much money is in your purse?"

"Forty gold pieces," replied the knight.

Robin took the forty pounds and counted it. One half he gave to his men and told them to drink to the King's health with it. The other half he handed back to the knight.

"Sir," said he courteously, "have this for your spending. If you live with kings and lords, you will need it."

"Grammercy!" replied the other smiling.

Then Robin walked on one side of the knight's steed and Friar Tuck on the other till they came to the open glade before the caves of Barnesdale. Then Robin drew out his bugle and sounded the three signal blasts of the band. Soon there were more than a hundred yeomen in sight. All were dressed in new suits of Lincoln green and carried new bows in their hands and bright short swords at their belts. And every man bent his knee to Robin Hood before taking his place at the tables, which were already set.

A handsome page stood at Robin's right hand to pour his wine and that of the knight. The knight marvelled at all he saw and said to himself: "These men of Robin Hood's give him more obedience than my fellows give me."

At the signal from Robin, the dinner began. There was venison and fowl and fish and wheat cakes and ale and red wine in great plenty, and it was a good sight to see the smiles upon the hungry men's faces.

First they listened to a grace from Friar Tuck, and then Robin lifted high a tankard of ale.

"Come, let us now begin," said he. "In honor of our guest who comes with a royal message, here's to the health of the King!"

The guest responded heartily to this toast and

the men cheered noisily for King Richard!

After the feast was over, Robin turned to his guest and said: "Now you shall see what life we lead, so that you may report faithfully, for good or bad, unto the King."

At a signal from him, the men rose up and smartly bent their bows for practice. The knight was greatly astonished at the smallness of their targets. A branch was set up, far down the glade, and a garland of roses was balanced on it. Whoever failed to send his shaft through the garland, without knocking it off the branch, would be struck by the hand of Friar Tuck.

"Ho, ho!" cried the knight, as his travelling companion rose up and bared his brawny arm, "so you, my friend, are Friar Tuck!"

"I have not denied it," replied Tuck, growling at having betrayed himself. "But chastisement is a rule of the church, and I am seeking the good of these stray sheep."

David of Doncaster shot first and landed safely through the rose garland. Then came Allan-a-Dale and Little John and Stutely and Scarlet and many of the rest. The knight held his breath from amazement. Each fellow shot truly through the garland, until Middle, the tinker, stepped up for a trial. But while he made a fair shot for a townsman, the arrow flew outside the rim of the garland.

"Come here, fellow," said Little John coaxingly. "The priest will bless thee with his open hand."

Then, because Middle made a sorry face and loitered in his steps, Arthur-a-Bland and Will Stutely seized him by the arms and stood him before the friar. Tuck's big arm flashed through the air —"whoof!"— Middle himself went rolling over and over on the grass. He was stopped by a small bush and he sat up, rubbing his ear. The merry men roared, and the knight laughed till tears rolled down his face.

After Middle's bad luck, others of the band fared in the same fashion. The garland would topple over even though the arrows went through it. So Middle began to feel better when he saw these others also tumbling on the grass.

At last came Robin's turn. He shot carefully, but as luck would have it, the shaft was badly feathered and swerved sidewise so that it missed the garland. Then a great roar went up from the whole company. It was rare that they saw their leader miss his mark. Robin flung his bow upon the ground from irritation.

"The arrow was sadly winged!" he complained. "I felt the poor feather upon it as it left my fingers!"

Then suddenly picking up his bow again, he sped three shafts as fast as he could send them and every one went clean through the garland.

"By Saint George!" muttered the knight. "I never before saw such shooting in all Christendom!"

The band cheered heartily at these last shots, but Will Scarlet came up gravely to Robin.

"Pretty shooting, master!" said he, "but it will not save you from paying for the bad arrow. So walk up and take your medicine!"

"No, that may not be!" protested Robin. "The good friar belongs to my company and has no authority to lift his hand against me. But you, Sir Knight, stand for the King. I pray you, serve out my blow."

"Not so!" said Friar Tuck. "My son, you forget I stand for the church, which is even greater than the King."

"Not this day," said the knight in a deep voice. Then rising to his feet, he added: "I stand ready to serve you, Robin Hood."

"Upstart knight!" cried Friar Tuck. "I told you last night, sir, that we should yet see who was the better man! So we will prove it now, and thus settle who is to pay Robin Hood."

"Good!" said Robin. "I do not want to start a dispute between church and state."

"Good!" also said the knight. "Come, friar, strike if you dare. I will give you first blow."

"You have the advantage of an iron pot on your head and gloves on your hands," said the friar, "but down you shall go, even if you were **Goliath**."

GOLIATH
The giant warrior of the Philistines whom David, the youthful champion of the Israelites, killed with a stone thrown from a sling.

Once more the priest's brawny arm flashed through the air, and struck with a "whoof!" But to the amazement of all, the knight did not budge from his tracks, though the upper half of his body twisted slightly to ease the force of the blow.

GAUNTLET
A glove with armor protecting the hand.

"Now my turn," said the knight coolly, casting aside his **gauntlet**. And with one blow of his fist the knight sent the friar

Merry·Robin·
hath·the·
worst·of·
a·
Bargain·

spinning to the ground.

If there had been uproar before, it was as nothing to the noise which now broke forth. Every fellow held his sides from laughter—every fellow, except one, and that was Robin Hood.

Out of the frying pan into the fire! he thought. He wished he had let the friar box his ears, after all!

Robin's plight was indeed a sorry one, and now the knight turned on him and sent him tumbling head over heels. But Robin was spared the laughter of the merry men by an unexpected event. A horn sounded in the glade and a party of knights was seen approaching.

"To arms!" cried Robin, hurriedly seizing his sword and bow.

"It's Sir Richard of the Lea!" cried another, as the troop came nearer.

And so it was. Sir Richard spurred his horse forward and dashed into the camp. Near the spot where the Black Knight stood, he dismounted and knelt before him.

"I trust Your Majesty has not needed our help," he said humbly.

"'Tis the King!" cried Will Scarlet, falling to his knees, too.

"The King!" echoed Robin Hood after a pause of amazement. And he and all his men bent reverently on their knees.

CHAPTER 20

How Robin Hood And Maid Marian Were Wed

"'Stand up again,' then said the King,
   'I'll thee thy pardon give;
Stand up, my friend; who can contend,
   When I give leave to live?'
      ......
"Then Robin Hood began a **health**
   To Marian, his only dear;
And his yeoman all, both comely and tall,
   Did quickly bring up the rear."

YOUR PARDON, SIRE!" exclaimed Robin Hood.
"Pardon these, my men, who stand ready to
serve you all your days!"

Richard the Lion Hearted looked grimly
about over the kneeling band.

HEALTH
A drinking
toast wishing
for health.

"Is it as your leader says?" he asked.

"Aye, my lord King!" burst from all throats at once.

"We are not outlaws from choice alone," continued Robin, "but have been driven to it by injustice. Grant us forgiveness and royal protection, and we will forsake the forest and follow the King."

Richard's eyes sparkled as he looked from one to another of this proud band, and he thought to himself that here, indeed, was a royal bodyguard worth having.

"Swear!" he said in his full rich voice; "swear that you, Robin Hood, and all your men from this day forward will serve the King!"

"We swear!" came the answering shout.

"Arise, then," said King Richard. "I give you all free pardon and will soon put your service to the test. I love such archers as you have shown yourselves to be. But, in truth, I cannot allow you to roam in the forest and shoot my deer. Nor to take the law of the land into your own hands. Therefore, I now appoint you to be Royal Archers and my own special bodyguard. There are one or two matters to settle with certain noblemen, in which I need your aid. Thereafter, half of you shall come back to these woodlands as Royal Foresters. May you show as much zeal in protecting my preserves as you have shown in hunting them. Where, now, is that outlaw known as Little John?"

"Here, sire," said the giant, raising his cap.

"Good master Little John," said the King, looking him over approvingly. "You are this day made Sheriff of Nottingham, and I trust you will make a better official than the man you relieve."

"I shall do my best, sire," said Little John, with great astonishment and gladness in his heart.

"Master Scarlet, stand forth," said the King, and then addressing him: "I have heard your tale," said he. "Your father was the friend of my father. Now, therefore, accept the royal pardon and resume possession of your family estates. And come to London next Court day and we shall see if there is a knighthood vacant."

Likewise the King called for Will Stutely and made him Chief of the Royal Archers. Then he summoned Friar Tuck to draw near.

"I crave my King's pardon," said the priest, humbly enough, "for who am I to lift my hand against the King?"

"Nay, the Lord sent punishment to thee without delay," answered Richard, smiling. "So what can I do for you in payment of last night's hospitality? Can I find some fat living where there are no wicked men to reform and where the work is easy and comfortable?"

"I wish only for peace in this life," replied Tuck. "Mine is a simple nature and I care not for the **fripperies** and follies of court life. Give me a good meal, a cup of ale, and health, and I ask no more."

FRIPPERIES
Showy but foolish or useless things.

Richard sighed. "You ask the greatest thing in the world, brother—contentment. It is not mine to give or to deny. But ask your God for it, and if He grant it, then ask for it also for your King." He glanced around once more at the foresters. "Which one of you is Allan-a-Dale?" he asked. And when Allan had come forward: "So," said the King with sober face, "you are that minstrel who stole a bride at Plympton church. I heard something of this. Now what excuse have you to make?"

"Only that I love her, sire, and she loves me," said Allan, simply. "And the Norman lord would have married her to have her lands."

"From tomorrow you and Mistress Dale are to

return to them and live in peace and loyalty," said the King. "And if ever I need your harp at Court, be ready to serve me and bring also the lady. Speaking of ladies," he continued, turning to Robin Hood, who had stood silent, wondering if a special punishment was being reserved for him, "did you not have a sweetheart who was once at court—one Mistress Marian? What has become of her? Have you forgotten her?"

"No, Your Majesty," said the page, coming forward blushingly. "Robin has not forgotten me!"

"So!" said the King, bending to kiss her small hand gallantly. "As I have already thought to myself, this Robin Hood is better served than the King in his palace! But are you not the only child of the late Earl of Huntingdon?"

"I am, sire, though there be some who say that Robin Hood's father was the rightful Earl of Huntingdon. Nonetheless, neither he is advantaged nor I, for the estates are taken from us."

"Then they shall be restored!" cried the King. "And to keep you two from your families' ancient quarrel over them, I bestow them upon you jointly. Come forward, Robin Hood."

Robin came and knelt before his king. Richard drew his sword and touched him upon the shoulder.

"Rise, Robin Fitzooth, Earl of Huntingdon!" he exclaimed, while a mighty cheer arose from the band. "The first command I give you, my lord Earl," continued the King when quiet was restored, "is to marry Mistress Marian without delay."

"May I obey all Your Majesty's commands as willingly!" cried the new Earl of Huntingdon, drawing the old Earl's daughter close to him. "The ceremony shall take place tomorrow, if this maid is willing."

"She makes no protest," said the King, "so I shall give away the bride myself!"

Then the King chatted with others of the foresters and made himself one of them for the evening, rejoicing in the freedom of the woods. As the shades of night drew on, the whole company—knights and foresters—supped and drank round a blazing fire, while Allan sang sweetly to the strumming of the harp, and the others joined in the chorus.

It was a happy, carefree night, this last one together under the greenwood tree. Robin could not help feeling sadness that it was to be the last. But he knew it was better so, and that the new life with Marian and in the service of his King would bring its own joys.

Then the night deepened, the fire sank, and the company lay down to rest. The King, at his own request, spent the night in the open, and thus they all slept out under the stars.

IN THE MORNING the whole company was early on its way to Nottingham. Outside the gates they were halted.

"Who comes here?" asked the guard's surly voice.

"Open to the King of England!" came back the clear answer, and the gates were opened and the bridge let down without delay.

Almost before the company had crossed the moat the news spread through the town like wildfire.

"The King is here! The King is here—and has taken Robin Hood!"

From every corner the people flocked to see the company pass. They cheered wildly for the King, who rode smilingly through the marketplace.

At the far end of it he was met by the Sheriff, who came up puffing in his haste to do the King honor. He fairly turned green with rage when he saw Sir Richard of the Lea and Robin Hood in the royal company, but he made a low bow to his master.

"Sir Sheriff," said the King, "I have rid the shire of outlaws, according to my promise. There are none left, for they all are now in the service of their King. I have determined to place in charge of this shire a man who fears no other man in it. Little John is hereby created Sheriff of Nottingham, and you will turn over the keys to him forthwith."

The Sheriff bowed, but dared not speak. Then the King turned to the Bishop of Hereford, who had also come up to pay his respects.

"Hark, my lord Bishop," he said, "the stench of your evil actions has reached our nostrils. We shall demand strict accounting for certain seizures of lands and certain acts of oppression that ill become a man of the church. But first, this afternoon you must perform at the wedding of two of our company in Nottingham Church. So make ready."

The Bishop also bowed and departed, glad to escape a stronger punishment for the time being.

The company then rode on to the Mansion House, where the King received the townspeople until noon and the whole town made a holiday.

In the afternoon, the way from the Mansion House to Nottingham Church was lined with cheering people, as the wedding party passed by. Robin, who had long been secretly liked, was now doubly popular since he had the King's favor.

Along the way, ahead of the King and the smiling bride and groom, ran little maids strewing flowers. The only hearts that were not glad this day were those of the old Sheriff and of his proud daughter, who peered between the shutters of her window with envy and hatred.

Within the church they found the Bishop in his robes and by his side Friar Tuck, who had been especially asked to assist. The service was said in Latin, while the organ pealed softly. The King gave away the bride, and

Robin and Marian passed out again through the church doors as man and wife, while the greenwood men ran ahead and flung gold pennies right and left to the cheering crowds. Then the whole party went down to Gamewell Lodge, and thus, amid feasting and rejoicing and kingly favor, Robin Hood, the new Earl of Huntingdon, and his bride began their wedded life.

CHAPTER 21

How Robin Hood Met His Death

*"Give me my bent bow in my hand,
And a broad arrow I'll let flee;
And where this arrow is taken up,
There shall my grave digg'd be."*

R OBIN HOOD AND HIS MEN, now the Royal Archers, went with King Richard the Lion Hearted through England settling private disputes that had arisen while the King was gone to the Holy Land. Then the King proceeded amid great pomp and rejoicing to the palace at London, and Robin, the new Earl of Huntingdon, brought his Countess there, where she became one of the finest ladies of the court.

The Royal Archers were now divided into two

bands; one half of them remained in London, while the other half returned to Sherwood to guard the King's preserves.

Months passed by, and Robin began to tire of the customs of city life. He longed for the fresh air of the greenwood and the merry society of his yeomen. One day, seeing some lads at archery practice, he could not help but say: "Woe is me! I fear my hand is fast losing its old skill at the bowstring!"

Finally he asked leave to travel in foreign lands, and this was granted to him. He took Maid Marian with him, and together they went through many strange countries. Finally, in an Eastern land, Marian sickened of a plague and died. They had been married only five years, and Robin felt as though all the light was gone out from his life.

He wandered about the world for a few months longer, trying to forget his grief, then came back to the court at London and sought some commission in active service. But, unluckily, Richard was gone again on his adventures and Prince John, who acted as Regent during the King's absence, had never been fond of Robin. He received him with a sarcastic smile.

"Go into Sherwood Forest," said he coldly, "and kill some more of the King's deer. Perhaps then the King will make you Prime Minister, at the very least, upon his return."

The taunt fired Robin's blood. He had been in a black mood ever since his dear wife's death. He answered Prince John hotly, and the Prince ordered his guards to seize Robin and cast him into the **Tower**.

After lying there for a few weeks, he was released by the faithful Will Stutely and the Royal Archers and all together they fled to the greenwood. There Robin blew the old familiar call, which all had known and loved so well. Up came running the remainder of the band, who had been Royal Foresters, and when they saw their old master they embraced him and nearly cried for joy that he had come again to them. All renounced their loyalty to Prince John and lived quietly with Robin in the greenwood, harming no one and only waiting for the day when King Richard would come home again.

TOWER
The Tower of London is the city's ancient fortress, built on Roman foundations. Once the king's home, it was later used mainly as a jail for famous prisoners.

But King Richard did not come and would never need his Royal Guard again. News reached them of how he had met his death in a foreign land and how John reigned as King. The proof of these events followed soon after, when there came striding through the glade the big, familiar form of Little John.

"Are you come to arrest us?" called out Robin, as he ran forward and embraced his old comrade.

"Nay, I am not the Sheriff of Nottingham, thank God," answered Little John. "The new King has removed me, and it is greatly to my liking, for I have long desired to join you here again in the greenwood."

The new King waged war upon the outlaws soon after this, and he sent so many scouting parties into Sherwood that Robin and his men left the woods for a time and went into Derbyshire.

But in one of the last skirmishes Robin was wounded. The cut did not seem serious and healed over the top, but it left a lurking fever. Daily his strength ebbed away from him, until he was in sore distress.

One day as he rode along on horseback, near Kirklees Abbey, he became so faint that he reeled and came near falling from his saddle. He dismounted weakly and knocked at the abbey gate. A woman shrouded in black peered out.

"Who are you that knock here? For we allow no man within these walls," she said.

"Open, for the love of Heaven!" he begged. "I am Robin Hood, ill of a fever and in sore need of help."

At the name of Robin Hood the woman stepped back and then, after a pause, unbarred the door and admitted him. Assisting his fainting frame up a flight of stairs and into a front room, she loosened his collar and bathed his face until he was revived. Then she spoke hurriedly in a low voice:

"Your fever will sink, if you are **bled**. I will open your veins while you lie quiet."

So she bled him, and he fell into a sleep that lasted nearly all that day; he awoke weak and exhausted from loss of blood.

Some say this abbess who bled him did it in all kindness of heart. Others say that she was none other than the former

BLED
Medieval doctors believed that illnesses were caused by an imbalance among four fluids in the body. They cut open certain veins (depending on the sickness) and drained away blood, checking it for odor and greasiness, in order to restore balance.

Sheriff's daughter and found her revenge at last in this cruel deed.

Be that as it may, Robin's eyes swam from weakness when he awoke. He called wearily for help, but there

So. Yᵉ GREAT·REAPER·reapeth·
among·the·FLOWERS :⠂   ᴴᴾ

was no response. He looked longingly through the window at the green of the forest, but he was too weak to make the leap that would be needed to reach the ground.

He then thought of his horn, which hung at his knee, and blew out three weak blasts."

Little John was out in the forest nearby, or the notes would never have been heard. At their sound he sprang to his feet.

"Woe! Woe!" he cried, "I fear my master is near dead, he blows so wearily!"

So he came running up to the door of the abbey and knocked loudly. Failing to get a reply, he beat in the door with frenzied blows of his mighty fist and soon came running up to the room where Robin lay, white and faint.

"Alas, dear master!" cried Little John in great distress, "I fear you have met with treachery! If that be so, grant me one last favor, I pray."

"What is it?" asked Robin.

"Let me burn Kirklees Hall with fire, and all its nunnery."

"No, good comrade," answered Robin Hood gently, "I cannot grant such a request. We must forgive all our enemies. Moreover, you know I never hurt a woman in all my life, nor any man when in a woman's company."

He closed his eyes and fell back, so that his friend thought he was dying. Great tears fell from the giant's eyes and wet his master's hand. Robin slowly rallied and seized his comrade's outstretched arm.

"Lift me up, good Little John," he said brokenly. "Give me my good yew bow and fix a broad arrow upon the string. Out yonder among the oaks—where this arrow falls—let them dig my grave."

And with one last mighty effort he sped his shaft out the open window, straight and true, as in the days of old, till it struck the largest oak of them all and dropped in the shadow of the trees. Then he fell back upon the sobbing chest of his devoted friend.

Robin·shooteth·his·Last·Shaft:

"This is the last!" he murmured. "Tell the brave hearts to lay me with my bent bow at my side, for it has made sweet music in my ears."

Then all of a sudden Robin's eye brightened, and he seemed to think he was back once more with the band in the open forest glade. He struggled to rise.

"Ha! a fine stag, Will! And Allan, never did you strum the harp more sweetly. How the fire blazes! And Marian! My Marian—come at last!"

So died Robin Hood, but his spirit lives on through the centuries in the hearts of men who love freedom and chivalry.

They buried him where his last arrow had fallen and set up a stone to mark the spot. On the stone were carved these words:

"HERE UNDERNEATH THIS LITTLE STONE
LIES ROBERT, EARL OF HUNTINGDON;
NEVER ARCHER AS HE SO GOOD,
AND PEOPLE CALLED HIM ROBIN HOOD.
SUCH OUTLAWS AS HE AND HIS MEN
ENGLAND WILL NEVER SEE AGAIN."